Contents

Introduction to

The Dominican Republic

The lush, sun-speckled Dominican Republic is the most popular tourist destination in the Caribbean. Prime beachfront stretches along the coast of the verdant island it shares with Haiti, some of it lined with mega-resorts and other facilities to handle the crowds, but much of it still remote and unspoiled. Short, inexpensive flights from the US coupled with cheap all-inclusive packages from Europe – added to the low cost of living in the country – make it an easy choice for a carefree, tropical holiday.

▲ La Vega Carnival

Even if you head to the most developed areas, in the Southeast around Punta Cana and Bávaro, or to the deluxe all-inclusives at Playa Dorada near Puerto Plata, you probably won't be disappointed – after all, these places weren't picked out of a hat. The white-sand beaches and crystal-clear waters are as splendid as any in the entire Caribbean.

When to visit

The Dominican Republic is blessed with a year-round tropical climate. Temperatures hover around 27°C (81°F) in summer, and 24°C (75°F) in winter; in the mountains, temperatures run about four degrees cooler on average, and on rare occasions it can drop below freezing. High seasons are from July to August and again from December through late February, when the climate has cooled down just a bit, making it the optimum time to visit. You'll save money – and have an easier time booking a hotel on the spot – during spring and fall. Prime hurricane season hits in August and September, but storms can occur in the months before or after as well.

▲ Los Haitises mangrove swamps

But the DR, as it's frequently called, boasts plenty more. Its storied history as the first European settlement in the New World remains a point of pride and can be seen to best effect in the well-preserved colonial district of the capital Santo Domingo and the ruins of Columbus's first colony, La Isabela. It's set on the most geographically diverse Caribbean island, with everything from towering pine-forested mountains dotted with crashing waterfalls and foaming whitewater rapids to nature preserves filled with mangrove swamps and wildlife habitats.

You'll have no problem accessing it all, whether you arrive in the capital or at Puerto Plata, on the north coast; both spots

▲ Las Terrenas

are plenty atmospheric on their own and worth a day or two of exploration, but can also be used as springboards for exploring the nearby coasts or the more rugged and rural interior.

In those regions, outdoor activities abound, from windsurfing at Cabarete to trekking in the pristine alpine wilderness of the Cordillera Central, which has the highest mountains east of the Mississippi River. Meanwhile, the gorgeous Samaná Peninsula not only draws scores of sun-worshippers, but thousands of humpback whales that pass by every winter.

Though many of the resorts are cut strictly from the Caribbean cloth, the Dominican Republic feels more a part of the pan-Latin culture that stretches from Texas to the tip of Tierra del Fuego. Spanish is pretty much the sole language spoken outside the resort areas, and the food is a relatively straightforward blend of Spanish, Taino (pre-Columbian natives) and African influences. It may not be overly exotic, but sitting by the ocean with a rum drink while merengue thrums from a nearby beach stand or boom box could just be all the excitement you need.

▲ Boca Chica

The **Dominican Republic**
AT A GLANCE

Santo Domingo

The first city built by Europeans in the New World retains much of its original architecture in the charming Zona Colonial, while the vibrant modern city buzzes at the frenetic pace of a Caribbean capital.

The Southeast

Due east of Santo Domingo, the gorgeous Southeast Coast offers both serene, unspoiled beaches and mammoth tourist resorts, plus the mangroves and rainforest of Parque Nacional Los Haitises.

▲ Rocky cliffs on the Samaná Peninsula

The Northeast Coast

Sun-washed stretches of sand line the Northeast Coast, most memorably at the windsurfing and surfing hotspot of Cabarete and the inviting fishing village of Río San Juan.

Puerto Plata and Playa Dorada

The coastal city of Puerto Plata hums with a lively local street life and provides a gateway – and antidote – to the walled-off tropical playland of Playa Dorada. The flat-topped Mount Isabela towers over them both.

▲ Surfing off the Northeast Coast

Samaná Peninsula

The island's most beautiful beaches unfold along this small peninsula, which in winter sees tens of thousands of humpback whales. The beach towns of Las Terrenas and Las Galeras provide welcoming bases.

The Northwest Coast

Rural and remote, this stretch of the island is populated largely by campesinos and herds of goats, making for a welcome change of pace if you're in need of it.

Santiago

The ever-expanding concrete metropolis of Santiago sees little tourist traffic but does have some pretty parks, nice markets, engaging museums and a happening nightlife. This is the hub of the Dominican tobacco industry.

The Cordillera Central

The Caribbean's highest peaks loom within the Cordillera Central, large portions of which are improbably blanketed in alpine vegetation that wouldn't look out of place in Switzerland. It's the place to go for serious hiking.

The Southwest

The semi-arid Southwest is economically backward but awash in natural beauty, particularly along the majestic coastline west of Barahona, the area's largest town.

▲ Cordillera Central

Ideas

The big six

Thanks to a diverse geography and rich colonial heritage, the Dominican Republic offers far more than sun-kissed beaches and a year-round tropical climate. A tour of these six sights will take you to all corners of the country, from the historic architecture of Santo Domingo and the sky-high, pine-covered Cordillera Central peaks to the spectacular coastline of the Southeast.

▼ The Cordillera Central

Untrammelled mountain wilderness awaits you in the island's verdant core.

P.140 ▶ THE CORDILLERA CENTRAL

▼ Ocean World

Interact with dolphins, seals and stingrays – and even tigers, piranhas and sharks – at the world-class marine park.

P.114 ▶ PUERTO PLATA AND PLAYA DORADA

▲ The Zona Colonial

Founded by Christopher Columbus and his family, the first European colony of the New World lies magically intact along the Río Ozama within modern Santo Domingo.

P.51 ▸ SANTO DOMINGO

▼ Samaná whales

Thousands of humpbacks arrive each winter to breed and give birth in the Bay of Samaná, making for the best whale-watching in the Caribbean.

P.87 ▸ SAMANÁ PENINSULA

▼ Lago Enriquillo

This serene salt-water lake the size of Manhattan teems with wildlife from swarms of birds to crocodiles and iguanas.

P.157 ▸ THE SOUTHWEST

▲ Playa Punta Cana

The world's most popular all-inclusive resort lies on a stunningly beautiful sandy beach along the Southeast Coast.

P.75 ▸ THE SOUTHEAST

Beaches

Most visitors come to bask on the country's archetypal Caribbean beaches – breathtaking strands of soft white sand, lapped by turquoise waters and lined with swaying palm trees. You'll find swaths of coast to suit all tastes, from super-developed tourism centres to lively locals-only hang-outs to utterly remote and unspoiled patches of tranquillity.

▲ Playa Punta Cana

Soak up rays on the silky sand and then frolic in the aquamarine waters at this sublime spot.

P.75 ▸ THE SOUTHEAST

▶ Playa Bonita

The most beautiful Dominican beach bar none, fairly isolated but with a handful of independent hotels – the ultimate in serenity and natural splendour.

P.89 ▶ SAMANÁ PENINSULA

◀ Playa Dorada

Fun, frenetic environment full of foreign sunworshippers, hair braiders, group aerobics and the like.

P.112 ▶ PUERTO PLATA AND PLAYA DORADA

▶ Playa Rincón

If you're industrious enough to get out to the tip of the Samaná Peninsula, you'll have this remote, sandy beach all to yourself.

P.88 ▶ SAMANÁ PENINSULA

◀ Playa Sosúa

Lively Playa Sosúa is ideal for sunning and swimming, followed by a cold beer at one of the many makeshift beach bars.

P.98 ▶ THE NORTHEAST COAST

Bars and lounges

Dominican bar life traditionally centres around the national beer, Presidente, which is kept so ice-cold that it may be a solid rather than a liquid if you don't rub the bottom of the bottle before popping the cap. You'll find plenty of quirky, social spots to imbibe that – and the odd tropical concoction – all across the country.

▲ **Daiqui Loco**

On Santiago's main drag, this locally famous outdoor bar offers frozen daiquiris and margaritas – and the best people-watching in town.

P.138 ▸ SANTIAGO AND AROUND

▲ Hemingway's Bar & Grill

Playa Dorada's party bar is always packed with tipsy foreigners committing karaoke and engaging in general mayhem.

P.118 ▶ PUERTO PLATA AND PLAYA DORADA

▶ Atarazana 9

Owned by famed bachata and merengue crooner Juan Luís Guerra, this hip Santo Domingo joint jams with alternative Latin garage bands.

P.67 ▶ SANTO DOMINGO

▼ Onno's

Kick back at this lively, open-air Cabarete beachfront lounge that really gets going in the wee hours.

P.106 ▶ THE NORTHEAST COAST

Outdoor adventures

Outdoor enthusiasts are in luck. The DR offers an abundance of adventure options, both on land and sea. Hike, bike or horse-ride through the country's remarkably diverse terrain – from stark desert to dense rainforest – or explore swamps and sea by boat.

▲ Horse-riding to El Limón waterfall

Embark on a three-hour ride through the palm-thick Samaná foothills to a stunning 150-metre waterfall cascading down a sky-high cliff.

P.89 ▸SAMANÁ PENINSULA

▲ Exploring Taino caves

The Dominican Republic is pocked with eerie caves, many of which hold extensive Amer-indian rock art.

P.72 ▸THE SOUTHEAST

▶ Boat trips in Parque Nacional Los Haitises

Float into a snarl of limestone caves and otherworldy mangrove swamps that for centuries were the lair of pirates.

P.78 ▶ THE SOUTHEAST

◀ Hiking to Pico Duarte

Test your mettle hiking up the Caribbean's highest mountain, marked by a bust of the DR's founding father.

P.144 ▶ THE CORDILLERA CENTRAL

▶ Mountain biking in the Cordillera Septentrional

Pedal through the northern Cordillera Septentrional and its idyllic campos on a trip run by Iguana Mama, the island's premiere adventure tour operator.

P.101 ▶ THE NORTHEAST COAST

◀ Whale watching in Samaná

Excellent whale-watching tours offer the rare chance to get an up-close look at these majestic creatures.

P.87 ▶ SAMANÁ PENINSULA

All-inclusive resorts

The Dominican Republic is known as the all-inclusive capital of the planet, and if you're in the mood to have all your needs catered for, you'll find plenty to fit the bill – especially around Playa Dorada, Punta Cana and Bávaro. Still, not all resorts are created equal; the following represent the cream of the crop. What you might lose in "authentic experience" you'll likely gain in relaxation.

▲ Ríu Resort

Relax amid palm-shaded cabañas and swimming pools dotted with artificial islands at this classy Julio Iglesias brainchild.

P.80 ▶ THE SOUTHEAST

▼ Gran Ventana

The meticulously groomed beachfront and grounds flourish with tropical gardens and Baroque fountains.

P.115 ▶ PUERTO PLATA AND PLAYA DORADA

▼ Bahía Príncipe

This massive all-inclusive boasts a private beach lined with outdoor bars, making for the best nightlife around.

P.107 ▶ THE NORTHEAST COAST

▲ Playa Esmeralda

Unwind at this quiet hotel with a soothing beach, grounds swarming with songbirds, and easy access to Santo Domingo.

P.80 ▶ THE SOUTHEAST

▼ Club Viva Dominicus

Set on one of the island's best beaches, the lavish compound offers private beach bungalows and great watersports.

P.79 ▶ THE SOUTHEAST

Colonial history

The Dominican Republic's colonial legacy dates back to the arrival of Columbus, who set up his base camp here and settled in as Spain's colonial administrator. In Santo Domingo's Zona Colonial, you can pick through sixteenth-century ruins and visit the New World's first cathedral, hospital, university, monastery and nunnery.

▲ Casa Francia on Calle de las Damas

Santo Domingo's pristinely preserved colonial thoroughfare holds many sixteenth-century architectural gems.

P.57 ▸ SANTO DOMINGO

▼ Fort San Felipe

Used as a prison during Trujillo's time, this sixteenth-century fort is now a well-preserved tourist attraction.

P.108 ▶ PUERTO PLATA AND PLAYA DORADA

▲ Casa Ponce de León

Tour the fortified home of the famed conquistador in pueblo San Rafael de Yuma.

P.75 ▶ THE SOUTHEAST

▶ Alcázar de Colón

The Columbus family palace stares proudly out over the port and old royal courts.

P.58 ▶
SANTO
DOMINGO

◀ Cathedral Santa María

The New World's first cathedral is a beauty, with Plateresque friezes along its western face.

P.54 ▶
SANTO
DOMINGO

Watersports

Playa Cabarete has become the Caribbean centre for watersports, due mainly to its ideal windsurfing and kitesurfing conditions. Diving on the island is not as popular as you might expect, as many of the local reefs are in bad condition, but the coast west of Puerto Plata still holds a thriving, tropical sea life. If you'd prefer to barrel down frothing river rapids, head to the waters that lace the interior mountain ranges.

▲ White-water rafting in Jarabacoa

Medium-level white-water rapids offer the chance to crash down scenic rivers in the central mountains.

P.141 ▶ THE CORDILLERA CENTRAL

▲ Kiteboarding in Cabarete

Easier to learn than windsurfing, kiteboarding has become equal in popularity, with a prestigious international competition held yearly.

P.100 ▶ THE NORTHEAST COAST

▼ Surfing at Playa Encuentro

The insanely high waves at Encuentro attract
hordes of half-suicidal surfers – and provide
thrills and spills during the famous
Encuentro Classic competition.

P.100 ▶ THE NORTHEAST COAST

▲ Diving in Monte Cristi

In addition to a dozen colonial-era shipwrecks, the waters here abound with healthy
reefs, a rarity in the Dominican Republic.

P.172 ▶ ESSENTIALS

▶ Windsurfing in Cabarete

Playa Cabarete boasts the
best windsurfing in the
Caribbean bar none, with
a dozen world-class outfits
dedicated to teaching the
crowds.

P.100 ▶ THE
NORTHEAST COAST

◀ Sportfishing on the Southeast Coast

Anglers battle marlin and
other trophy fish in the
teeming waters off the
Southeast Coast.

P.69 ▶ THE
SOUTHEAST

Museums

Spend some time museum going to enhance your understanding of local art and customs, as well as pre-Columbian history. The best known concerns itself with preserving the legacy of the native Taino Indians, who lived on the island before the Spanish conquest. You'll also find an excellent museum of twentieth-century Dominican art and one featuring the amber that inspired the movie *Jurassic Park*.

▲ Museo Folklórico Tomás Morel

Carnival masks from across the country are showcased at the quirky, fascinating Folklore Museum.

P.134 ▸ SANTIAGO AND AROUND

▶ Museo del Hombre Dominicano

The crown jewel of Dominican museums, this five-storey behemoth boasts two floors of Taino artefacts and a floor devoted to the country's African heritage.

P.61 ▶ SANTO DOMINGO

▲ Museo Ámbar

Housed in a nineteenth-century tobacco-farmer's mansion, the terrific Amber Museum displays animal and plant life preserved for tens of millions of years.

P.110 ▶ PUERTO PLATA AND PLAYA DORADA

▼ Museo Bellapart

This private collection includes many of the great masterpieces of early twentieth-century Dominican art, including José Vela Zanetti.

P.62 ▶ SANTO DOMINGO

Cuisine specialities

Dominican cuisine is typically starch-heavy, with rice and beans and *tostones* (fried plantains) playing a major part in just about every meal. Aside from these staples, you'll also find a number of delicious local specialities, including the locally grown, strong Dominican coffee, fresh shrimp in a fragrant garlic sauce, and *sancocho*, a savory national dish brought out for family celebrations.

▲ Camarones al ajillo

A light garlic sauce augments, but does not overwhelm, the exceptionally fresh local shrimp, best enjoyed in the coastal city of Barahona.

P.161 ▸ THE SOUTHWEST

▲ Café con leche

Sample the popular, delicious mix of espresso with steamed milk at Santo Domingo's bustling cafés.

P.66 ▸ SANTO DOMINGO

◀ Morir soñando

One sip of this heavenly concoction of orange juice, condensed milk, sugar and crushed ice and you'll understand why it's called "to die dreaming".

P.171 ▸ ESSENTIALS

▼ Langosta criolla

There are few other places in the world where you can get lobster caught the same day for as little as US$10; a spicy creole sauce adds just the right touch.

P.94 ▸ SAMANÁ PENINSULA

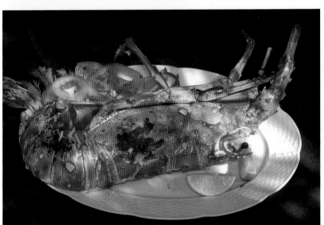

▶ Sancocho

The national delicacy, this hearty stew features five different kinds of meat, four types of root and a bewildering array of vegetables and spices.

P.171 ▸ ESSENTIALS

Natural Dominican Republic

The DR abounds with natural beauty, from placid lagoons with swarms of fluttering birds to tangled mangrove swamps and lush rainforests. It may occasionally involve a trek deep into the wilderness of an undervisited region to see the highlights, but the rewards are immense.

▲ The Cordillera Central

The verdant peaks of the Cordillera Central loom higher than the Appalachians in North America, and are protected by three massive national parks.

P.140 ▸ THE CORDILLERA CENTRAL

▶ Laguna Cabral

Flamingos, storks and other indigenous birds flock to this idyllic lake.

P.157 ▶ THE SOUTHWEST

◀ Los Haitises National Park

Float past craggy islands and impenetrable mangrove swamps in this otherworldly national park.

P.78 ▶ THE SOUTHEAST

▶ Lago Enriquillo

In the centre of placid Lago Enriquillo sits a sandy island teeming with rhinoceros iguanas.

P.157 ▶ THE SOUTHWEST

◀ Redondo and El Limón lagoons

Glide along the waters of these twin lagoons chock-full of birdlife.

P.77 ▶ THE SOUTHEAST

Dominican beat

Most of the happening nightlife in the country revolves around Latin music. For the best in traditional live sounds, head to one of the capital's charmingly old-fashioned son clubs. You'll also find a slew of popular discos across the island where you can groove to merengue and bachata. More contemporary offerings include a thriving rave scene at Santo Domingo's trendier nightspots.

▲ La Guácara Taina

Set in a multi-storey underground cave once used by the Tainos for religious ceremonies, this club has undergone a renaissance as a major rave spot.

P.68 ▶ SANTO DOMINGO

▲ La Barrica

Catering mostly to indigenous city-dwellers, this hip merengue club has no lights whatsoever and the waiters use flash-lights to take your order.

P.119 ▶ PUERTO PLATA AND PLAYA

▶ Nuevo Mundo

Just off pretty Playa Las Terrenas, the happening *Nuevo Mundo* wouldn't look out of place in Tribeca, with tasty cocktails, great dancing and diverse music.

P.95 ▶ SAMANÁ PENINSULA

▼ Cubanía

The hottest Cuban musical stars perform in the courtyard of this converted sixteenth-century manor.

P.67 ▶ SANTO DOMINGO

▲ Monumento del Son

Tap your toes to son music at this old-school club, complete with a corny vaudeville ventriloquist-emcee.

P.68 ▶ SANTO DOMINGO

Local culture

Away from the resorts, you'll find plenty of opportunities to observe – and partake in – Dominican daily life, from the national passion for baseball and the omnipresent dance clubs and billiard rooms in every village to dramatic cockfights and weekend mob scenes at local swimming holes. It's no surprise to find Santo Domingo the centre for much of the action.

▲ Playa Boca Chica

Every weekend tens of thousands of Santo Domingans transform this seedy tourist trap into a boom-box-blaring party scene.

P.69 ▶ THE SOUTHEAST

▲ Baseball

Baseball is the national obsession, and the Dominican winter season offers the chance to see the big stars of tomorrow.

P.62 ▶ SANTO DOMINGO

▶ Cuban son clubs

For an authentic Buena Vista Social Club experience, cut moves to Cuban son music at the posh, old-fashioned clubs that ring the capital.

P.68 ▶ SANTO DOMINGO

▲ Santo Domingo Malecón

By day, take a relaxing stroll along the capital's oceanfront boardwalk; come night, get ready to party on what the *Guinness Book of World Records* calls "The World's Largest Disco".

P.60 ▶ SANTO DOMINGO

▼ Cockfighting arenas

Many outsiders find this spectacle too bloody, but Dominicans are crazy about cockfighting – if it doesn't offend your sensibilities, visit a local arena and see for yourself.

P.159 THE SOUTHWEST

Remote getaways

Few visitors make it to the somewhat isolated, beautiful spots listed here – and they're missing out. If you truly want to get away from it all, rent a car or join a tour to discover the country's hidden coastal and mountain getaways, from quiet, lush valleys to haunting desert landscapes.

▲ San Rafael and Los Patos

Ice-cold mountain water thrums into the sea at these twin waterfalls west of Barahona, both with popular swimming holes.

P.158 ▶ THE SOUTHWEST

▶ Boca de Yuma

Crashing surf along the high cliffs of this backwater town make for some of the island's most majestic views.

◀ San José de las Matas

Enjoy the crisp mountain air at this sleepy, idyllic outpost that serves as a popular starting point for treks to Pico Duarte.

▶ Constanza

In the heart of the Cordillera Central, this circular Shangri-la valley offers scenic views and memorable mountain hikes.

▼ Monte Cristi

The flat-topped El Morro mountain and austere desert beauty surrounds this frontier pueblo, with seven Robinson Crusoe islands in the bay.

Casual dining

Most traditional Dominican comedores serve a standard line-up of rice and beans, grilled chicken and fried fish with plantains. When done right, these dishes can hit the spot, but you'll find a plethora of other cheap and tasty eats to break the monotony of such a steady diet.

▲ Panadería Repostería Dick

Just the smells emanating from this fragrant bakery will give you a new lease on life – try gourmet breads, buttery croissants and a steaming *café crème*.

P.106 ▶ THE NORTHEAST COAST

▲ Cafe Cito

Carve into the best filet mignon in the country for a fraction of what you'd pay elsewhere, while relaxing in an archetypal Graham Greene setting.

P.117 ▶ PUERTO PLATA AND PLAYA DORADA

▶ Boca Yate

Tuck into tasty pastas and superb grilled fish at this colourful, inviting Boca Yate eatery.

P.81 ▸ THE SOUTHEAST

▼ Café de Paris

This French-run hang-out on the Samaná boardwalk serves up delicious pizzas and crepes amid a colourful Pop Art decor.

P.92 ▸ SAMANÁ PENINSULA

▲ Melo's Cafe

Start your day with a hearty American breakfast washed down with fresh fruit shakes at this unpretentious little diner.

P.162 ▸ THE SOUTHWEST

Indulgent Dominican Republic

The Dominican Republic may be known as a budget destination, but that doesn't mean you have to go without some pampering. Tucked away in isolated corners of the island where mass tourism has yet to take root are one-of-a-kind havens that can succor both body and spirit; there are some more obvious spots for leisurely pursuits such as golf.

▲ Blue Moon

Channel the spirit of the ancient Rajas at this isolated mountaintop compound where you can dine on delicious multi-course gourmet Indian dinners in an expansive tent.

P.102 ▸ THE NORTHEAST COAST

▶ Fior di Loto

Achieve inner peace at this small India-themed hotel featuring yoga, meditation, martial arts and massage, plus a hot tub and a very private sun deck.

P.79 ▸ THE SOUTHEAST

◀ Golf at Playa Grande

This world-class course boasts gorgeous, wide-open sea views from all of its holes.

P.174 ▸ ESSENTIALS

▶ Casa de Campo

Sprawling alongside the sea, this luxury resort's 7000 meticulously manicured acres of rolling hills encompass polo grounds, equestrian stables, golf courses, tennis and spa.

P.78 ▸ THE SOUTHEAST

▼ Villa Serena

Gaze out at the palm-lined beach and a small desert island from the wraparound verandah of this beautiful faux-Victorian mansion with a verdant tropical garden.

P.92 ▸ SAMANÁ PENINSULA

Crafts and souvenirs

For those wishing to bring home a locally made keepsake, the Dominican Republic offers a small but quality selection of arts and crafts. The premiere portable art pieces are ornate papier-mâché Carnival masks with bangles and bone (for the teeth). Other possible scores include vibrant Haitian paintings, quality rum, hand-rolled cigars, and jewellery made with semi-precious larimar or amber.

▲ **Haitian painting**

The lush, "naivist" Haitian art style is famous the world over – and you can't beat the prices at the local art galleries.

P.54 ▸ SANTO DOMINGO

▼ Cigars

Insiders know that Dominican cigars are even better than those from neighbouring Cuba.

P.131 ▶ SANTIAGO AND AROUND

▼ Larimar

Mined in the coastal mountains west of Barahona and on display at the Museo Larimar in Santo Domingo, this turquoise-coloured, semi-precious stone is shown off to great effect as jewellery.

P.55 ▶ SANTO DOMINGO

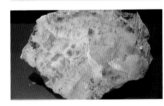

▼ Amber

Calcified tree sap the colour of caramel, amber is found in the hills north of Santiago.

P.135 ▶ SANTIAGO AND AROUND

▲ Carnival masks

The ultimate in Dominican folk art, this massive papier-mâché headgear is donned for Carnival every February across the country.

P.125 ▶ THE CORDILLERA CENTRAL

▲ Ron Añejo

Barceló and Brugal produce a high-quality, amber-coloured rum that's hard to find outside the Dominican Republic – and bearing it as a gift makes for a very popular homecoming.

P.112 ▶ PUERTO PLATA AND PLAYA DORADA

Resort day-trips

After a few days, the walled-in confines of an all-inclusive compound can feel like a vacation gulag. The easy answer is a trip to one of these nearby attractions, which will take you into the heart of the Dominican Republic and get you back in time for dinner.

▼ Damajagua cascades

Breathtaking cascades snake down the mountains outside of Puerto Plata.

P.114 ▶ PUERTO PLATA AND PLAYA DORADA

▼ Mount Isabela

Stunning views are just a dizzying cable-car ride away from Puerto Plata.

P.112 ▶ PUERTO PLATA AND PLAYA DORADA

◀ Macao

Just north of the Punta Cana and Bávaro resorts, but truly a world away, this unspoiled beach offers crashing waves and total isolation.

P.77 ▸ THE SOUTHEAST

▶ San Pedro Malecón

For Dominican street life at its best, stroll the waterfront promenade near Juan Dolio.

P.72 ▸ THE SOUTHEAST

◀ Cordillera Septentrional

From Río San Juan, explore the northern mountains where campesinos live much as they have for the past four hundred years.

P.96 ▸ THE NORTHEAST

▶ Isla Saona

Aquamarine waters lap the beaches of this uninhabited – though swarming with wildlife – island off the coast of Parque Nacional del Este near Bayahibe.

P.74 ▸ THE SOUTHEAST

Dominican oddities

Sometimes the best way to discover a culture is by seeking out its idiosyncrasies – and you don't have to go out of your way to find them in the DR. The need to stretch money as far as possible has led to a unique, antiquated transport system and nineteenth-century-style produce markets. Other peculiarities include a potent local drink made with rum and tree bark, and an ill-conceived eyesore of a monument.

▲ Mercado Hospidaje

Campesinos peddle the Cibao Valley's agricultural bounty at this sprawling open-air Santiago marketplace redolent of the nineteenth century.

P.134 ▶ SANTIAGO AND AROUND

▲ Guaguas

The unregulated nationwide network of battered minivans often seem held together with little more than packing tape and a strategically placed bit of rope.

P.51 ▸ SANTO DOMINGO

◀ MamaJuana

This hard-to-stomach concoction of local wines, rum, honey, and leaves and bark from various trees is said to prolong both sexual potency and life span.

P.171 ▸ ESSENTIALS

▼ Columbus Lighthouse

The bombastic multimillion-dollar complex spews a cross of light into the Santo Domingo night sky.

P.63 ▸ SANTO DOMINGO

Dominican calendar

The island's fiesta-heavy calendar means that on just about every day of the year you'll find a party in one town or another. These can range from traditional rural fiestas patronales in far-flung pueblos that have been celebrated for more than 200 years to high-octane merengue concerts showcasing internationally famous live acts.

▼ Virgen de Altagracia festival

The Higüey Basílica, topped with an imposing eighty-metre arch, draws tens of thousands of pilgrims who come to honour the country's patron saint on January 21.

P.75 ▶ THE SOUTHEAST

▼ Santo Domingo merengue festival

Virtually every famous merengue act from the last forty years – including Dominican merengue superstar Juan Luís Guerra – performs at this lively outdoor music festival in Santo Domingo on the last two weeks in July.

P.175 ▶ ESSENTIALS

▲ La Vega Carnival

La Vega throws the year's pre-eminent Carnival, held on every Sunday in February.

P.140 ▶ THE CORDILLERA CENTRAL

▶ Semana Santa festival in Cabral

Body-painted revellers dance through the streets of Cabral on Good Friday of Semana Santa (Holy Week).

P.174 ▶ ESSENTIALS

▼ New Year's Eve

An insane party atmosphere pervades the capital as the year winds down – the Malecón turns into a massive, mile-long discotheque, and well-known musical acts entertain the crowds.

P.60 ▶ SANTO DOMINGO

Places

Santo Domingo

Santo Domingo was the first European city founded in the New World – very much part of Columbus's legacy – and today serves as the modern face of the Dominican Republic. While it's crowded and industrial, the capital is also incredibly historic and boasts one of the Caribbean's liveliest waterfront boardwalks and a nightlife to match. Santo Domingo's colonial district, or Zona Colonial – which lies magically intact along the western bank of the Río Ozama – holds the first European cathedral, university, monastery, nunnery and hospital in the hemisphere. The historical bent continues at the museums of the Plaza de la Cultura; follow a visit there with a relaxing stroll through the rambling, residential district of Gazcue.

Puerta de la Misericordia

Hincado and Portes. A prime place to begin exploring the old city is at the massive Gate of Mercy, an early sixteenth-century fortified entrance that earned its name during the devastating earthquake of 1842, when local priests erected a tent city beneath it to treat the sick and shelter the homeless. Two years later, on February 27, 1844, freedom fighter Ramón Mella gave a dramatic speech here, inciting the city to insurrection, and fired off the first shot of the revolution against Haiti. A re-creation of the event is staged every Independence Day. Connected to the gate from the south are the rubble remains of its watchtower, the San Gil fort.

Puerta del Conde

Hincado and El Conde. An imposing stone structure adorned with a decorative, red-brick belfry, the Gate of the Count is where Ramón Mella raised the new

▲ ZONA COLONIAL AT NIGHT

Getting there and getting around

Most visitors arrive at Aeropuerto Internacional Las Américas (☎412-5888), the country's largest, 13km east of the city proper. From here you can take an RD$500 taxi into the city. There is no official public transport system in Santo Domingo, but the informal network of *públicos* and guaguas is a study in successful anarchy – they manage to cover every inch of the city and its outer districts and can get you pretty much anywhere for RD$20. Just stand on the corner of a major street and wave your arms at the first car with a taxi sign, provided you don't mind being crammed in with as many other people as can fit. If you want to use a private taxi, call Apolo (☎537-0000).

national flag for the first time. Named for Count Bernardo Bracamonte – whose military tactics saved the city from British invasion in 1655 – the gate leads into beautiful **Parque Independencia**, a popular meeting place encircled by a traffic-choked ring road, with shaded benches and a marker from which all distances in the capital are calculated. Near the park's centre is the honour-guarded **Altar de la Patria** (daily 8.30am–6pm; no shorts or short skirts; free), a marble mausoleum in which Mella is buried beside his compatriots Duarte and Sánchez.

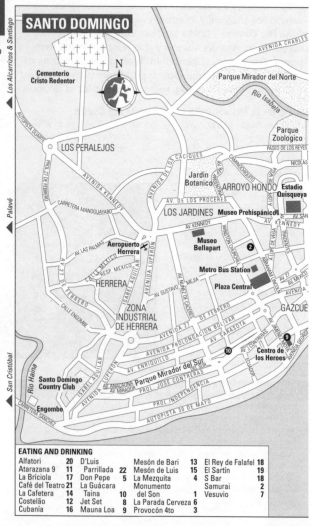

Calle El Conde

Lined with cafés, fast-food restaurants, clothing shops and bookstores, this broad pedestrian promenade is an ideal place to people watch, with hundreds of city-dwellers passing through at all hours and sidewalk vendors selling everything from pirated CDs to split coconuts.

Parque Colón

El Conde and Meriño. Crowds of locals spend their days in pleasant Parque Colón, conversing on the benches, playing dominoes and smoking cigars. Surrounded by beautiful colonial and Victorian buildings, the park holds a statue of Columbus in its centre. At the

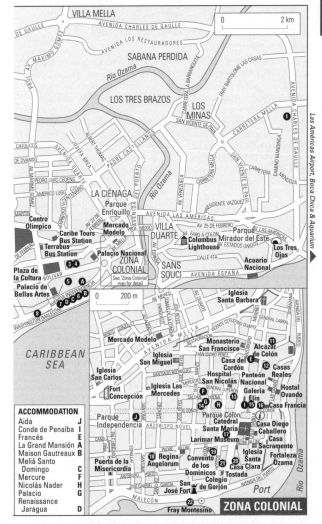

ACCOMMODATION

Aida	J
Conde de Penalba	I
Francés	E
La Grand Mansión	A
Maison Gautreaux	B
Meliá Santo Domingo	C
Mercure	F
Nicolás Nader	H
Palacio	G
Renaissance Jaragua	D

ZONA COLONIAL

▲ GALERÍA ELÍN

El Conde
at Parque
Colón. Daily
8am–4.30pm.
The imposing
Basílica
Catedral was
constructed
by the Vatican
to be the
religious
centre of the
West Indies
and the base for proselytizing
all the indigenous peoples of
the Americas. Built between
1521 and 1540, the exterior
actually bears little of the Gothic
influence that transformed sacred
architecture in Europe. The
western facade is Plateresque,
with an overabundance of friezes
and fanciful ornamentation, such
as the allegorical frieze above
the portals, showing a flight of
cherubs making their way past
horse-headed sea creatures and
impious women – meant to
symbolize the ocean journey of
the colonists.

Inside, under a Gothic ribbed
vault, are a seventeenth-century
marble altar and the Chapel
of Santa Ana, with the only
surviving original stained-glass
window, an angel hovering
over Virgin and Child. On the
northern wall you'll find the
Chapel of the Virgin of Antigua,
with its gorgeous groined vault
and a beautiful 1520 painting
of Mary, and the Chapel of
the Virgin of the Light, where
Columbus was interred for a
time.

west end rises the Victorian-
style nineteenth-century town
hall, no longer the seat of city
government but still used for
municipal office space, while to
the north sits a series of cigar
and souvenir shops, including
the **Museo de Ámbar**, El
Conde 107 (Mon–Sat 9am–
5pm; RD$30 museum entry), a
high-end jewellery store with
a small museum on the second
floor featuring ants, termites,
wasps and other insects trapped
in amber. On the park's east side
are Casa de Abogados, the old
town jail, and Palacio Borghella,
early nineteenth-century
buildings constructed by the
Haitians.

Galería Elín

Meriño 203. Mon–Sat 8am–5.30pm.
Spanning two buildings on
opposite sides of the street,
Galería Elín showcases an
incredible collection of the
very best Haitian art. Many of
the works are stacked up in
rows along the walls but don't
let the presentation fool you
– a walk through the shop
will give you an encyclopedic
survey of the history of Haitian
art, and the paintings here
cost less than half what they
would in the States or Western
Europe.

Iglesia Santa Clara

Billini and Isabela. The New
World's first nunnery and
another of the Catholic
institutions established in an

attempt to create a regional holy city, the largely unadorned Iglesia Santa Clara is often overlooked amid the imposing colonial monuments that surround it. Built in 1552, it was severely damaged by Drake and renovated by noted local businessman Rodrigo Pimentel. It's not officially open to the public, but can be explored on most weekdays, when it serves as a primary school.

Casa Sacramento

Isabela and Alfau. Built in 1520 by Diego Caballero, the peach-coloured Casa Sacramento was an important relic of the Church and now serves as the official residence of the archbishop. Renovations in the 1930s disguised its colonial bulk in a decorative Victorian wrap. You can walk through the two connecting courtyard gardens, or up to the viewing platforms or the towers, which offer scenic rooftop views of the neighbourhood.

Museo Larimar

Isabela 54 ☏689-6605. Mon–Sat 8am–6pm, Sun 8am–2pm. Free. Set in a remodelled late-colonial residence from the 1700s, the museum holds a variety of exhibits on larimar, a turquoise-coloured stone that exists only in the Dominican Republic. In addition to beautiful examples of raw larimar as it is mined from the Southwest's Bahoruco Mountains, the displays show how the semiprecious gem was created by local volcanic activity. You'll also learn to tell real from fake larimar, and there's of course a very nice jewellery shop on the ground floor; prices are comparable to what you'll find in other local souvenir shops, but the quality is higher.

Casa Tostado

Billini and Meriño ☏689-5057. Mon–Sat 9am–4pm. RD$10. Though Casa Tostada's most striking feature is the Gothic double window above the front door, the only one of its kind in this hemisphere, it's inside where you'll find what's of interest. There, the **Museum of the Nineteenth-Century Dominican Family** features a number of attractive (if unspectacular) antique furnishings, some Art Nouveau. Check out the geometric Mudéjar tiling on the courtyard well, and ask to climb the circular mahogany staircase that leads to the roof.

Colegio de Gorjón

Meriño and García. The sixteenth-century Colegio de Gorjón, the New World's second university, often houses contemporary art exhibits. Like all early colonial structures, the stonework was originally exposed, but in 1712 – under a misconception that the plague was transmitted through bare masonry – Philip V decreed that all buildings in the empire be plastered; this building is a beautifully whitewashed example. Check out as well the stunning courtyard on Calle García, with a delightful ocean view.

Calle de las Damas

The Street of the Ladies received its name in 1509, thanks to the retinue of women who would accompany Diego Columbus's wife María de Toledo down it to church every Sunday morning. Today it's traversed mostly by visitors who come for a look at the early sixteenth-century mansions that line the cobblestone blocks.

Fortaleza Ozama

Las Damas and Billini. Mon–Sat 9.30am–6pm, Sun 10am–3pm. RD$10. Long Santo Domingo's most strategic site, this is where Diego and María lived while their palace was under construction. Built in 1502 and enlarged over the centuries, it's set on a steep bank over the mouth of the Ozama and was the departure point for the Spanish conquests of Cuba, Colombia, Jamaica, Peru and Mexico – finally decommissioned after the American invasion of 1965. Beyond the Neoclassical main gate, the courtyard features a statue (with definite shades of Rodin) of González Oviedo, author of the first *History of the Indies* and commander of the fort from 1533 to 1557. The largest structure is the bulky medieval Torre de Homenaje, the most impenetrable part of the fortress and used for centuries as a prison. Climb to the top for panoramic views, or head inside where you'll find the hole through which prisoners on the grounds were dropped to their cells.

Casa Francia

Las Damas and El Conde. Mon–Fri 9am–5pm. Conquistador Hernán Cortes plotted his conquest of Mexico here, and you'll find his family's coat of arms in the second gallery. Note the parallel organization of arches on the first- and second-floor arcades, a departure from Spanish architectural tradition that was copied by later colonial houses. Beneath the ornament, though, these buildings were essentially fortified medieval keeps, reflecting the feudal aspirations of their owners.

Hotel Nicolás de Ovando

Las Damas and Mercedes. This hotel, which you can explore during the day (and stay in luxury at night; see p.64), incorporates the homes of the Ovando and Davila families, both prominent in the early colony. It's decorated with sixteenth-century furniture and a collection of medieval illuminated religious manuscripts illustrated in gold leaf, and so gives a good sense of colonial private life. Don't miss the double riverfront patio in the back, or the Davila coat of arms flanked by two griffins at the northernmost entrance. Attached to the hotel's north wall is **Capilla de los Remedios**, once the Davilas's private chapel, with an especially pretty triple-arched belfry atop its brick facade.

Panteón Nacional

Las Damas and Mercedes. Mon–Sat 9am–7pm. Free. The National Pantheon was built from 1714 to 1745 as a Jesuit convent. Today it's a nationalist monument where most of the major military and political figures from Dominican history are interred. The building's Neoclassical, martial facade seems particularly suited to its sober task, and is topped with a prominent cupola flanked by statues of Loyola and Jesus. The interior has been completely redone, with Italian marble floors, an enormous central chandelier donated by Spanish dictator Franco, and a massive central mausoleum.

Casa de las Gárgolas and Casa Viloria

Mercedes, off Las Damas. Five grimacing gargoyles stare down from the front door of Casa de las Gárgolas, their state of decay due in part to the vagaries of time, and in part to a seventeenth-century incident in which they were pelted with stones by a mob, who believed them supernaturally responsible for a series of local murders. One door over, Casa Viloria, built by the king's chamberlain Juan de Viloria in 1520, continues the supernatural theme, supposedly haunted by Viloria's ghost. Some locals claim that Viloria still appears one night a year and offers to reveal the location of his buried treasure to anyone willing to follow; apparently enough folks took up this offer to dig several holes in the courtyard's tile floor, found when work was begun on the house's restoration.

Plaza España

Las Damas and Tejera. The attractive, tiled Plaza España offers terrific views across the river, which you can enjoy from one of its many breezy outdoor cafés. The square was once the centre of colonial power and commerce, with sailors disembarking from the adjoining port, foreign merchants auctioning slaves, and Spain's high officials administering their empire from the Casas Reales. An intact section of the old town wall still skirts the plaza's eastern side, extending to **Puerta San Diego**, the colonial-era entrance from the port. More decorative than functionally defensive, its arcades are a favourite local hang-out;

on its eastern face you'll find **Parque Archeológico la Ceiba**, holding the excavated foundations of the colony's arrow-shaped, riverfront fort. At the centre stands a statue of Ovando and an eighteenth-century sundial on a pedestal, positioned so bureaucrats could tell the time by simply looking out the window.

Museo de las Casas Reales

Plaza España at Mercedes ☎682-4202. Tues–Sun 9am–6pm. RD$50. The Museum of Royal Houses, built between 1503 and 1520, functioned as the administrative centre of the West Indies, housing the Royal Court, Treasury, and Office of the Governor. The first-floor collection is a bit of a hodgepodge, with a few Taino artefacts, Spanish navigational instruments, slave shackles and an example of an old sugar mill. Near the back you'll find a rickshaw in which Spanish judges were carried to court by Tainos, and a sixteenth-century apothecary crammed with colourful glass vials. The second floor is more coherent, holding an armoury donated by Trujillo with examples of weaponry used here since Columbus, from chain mail and broadswords to Al Capone–style Tommy guns.

▲ CASA DE LAS GÁRGOLAS

PLACES Santo Domingo

Alcázar de Colón

Plaza España. Daily 9am–6pm. RD$50. Diego Columbus built the fortified Alcázar de Colón from 1511 to 1515, choosing this site because of its easy proximity to the Casas Reales, where he conducted official business, and so that it would be the first building seen by disembarking sailors and merchants. The mansion's portals are the finest local example of the late Gothic style called Isabelline, characterized by plain, linear surfaces adorned only with Islamic portals and delicate vine ornaments. Inside, a museum assembles an array of sixteenth-century pieces: reproductions of the stone gargoyles that held up the first-floor ceiling leer down at the collection of mahogany furniture, religious tapestries and period silverware. A second-floor private study showcases illuminated manuscripts from Spain and the music salon holds a sixteenth-century harp and clavichord. From the second floor you can walk to the terrace fortifications, the construction of which led Spanish officials to fear Diego intended to barricade his followers inside and declare himself "Emperor of the Americas".

Museo de las Atarazanas

Plaza España at Atarazana ☎682-4834. Daily 9am–5pm. RD$20. In the old days, the winding row of colonial storefronts known as Las Atarazanas held taverns frequented by passing mariners and also the city's large public market, where ships stocked up on tropical fruit to combat scurvy. Follow it to the end where the Reales Atarazanas, once the port authority, contains the colonial naval museum, with exhibits of recovered booty – coins, bars of silver, pottery – from the wreck of the sixteenth-century Spanish galleon *Concepción*, sunk during a hurricane in the Bahía de Samaná.

Casa del Cordón

Tejera and Isabela. The former home of Francisco de Garay (later a founder of Spanish Jamaica), the Isabelline Casa de Cordón was named for its portal, which features beautiful arabesque ornamentation and a giant, stone monk's belt from the Franciscan order hanging above it in imitation of an *arraba*, an Islamic rectangular portal frame. It's used as office space for Banco Popular, but the vine-covered courtyard with its Mudéjar-tiled staircase is open to visitors during the day.

Monasterio San Francisco

Tejera and Hostos. This 1544 Franciscan monastery weathered an artillery assault from Sir Francis Drake and the brunt of several earthquakes, which levelled the main building and the original chapel adjacent to it. Above the entrance are the curling stone belt of the Franciscan order and a Renaissance bust of Bishop Geraldini, who oversaw its initial construction. The Gothic portal below leads to the Chapel of the Third Order (an organization of spiritual laymen), built in 1704 after the original was flattened. The coral-pink arcade opens onto the cloisters and the monastery church – a popular spot for local weddings. The monastery was used as an insane asylum through the nineteenth century, and at points along the walls you'll see the metal studs that held inmates' leg chains.

Convento de los Dominicos

Billini and Duarte. The charming 1510 Convento de los Dominicos was home to the New World's first university, San Tomé de Aquino. Its striking stone facade is framed by decorative two-dimensional pillars; blue Mudéjar tiling runs along the top of the portal, and a profusion of red Isabelline vine ornamentation surrounds the circular window in the centre. Inside, on the vault of the sanctuary's Chapel of the Rosary (the first chapel to the right of the entrance) you'll find an impressive reminder that European Christianity was a syncretic religion long before it came to the New World: an enormous pagan zodiac wheel is guarded by Jupiter (spring), Mars (summer), Mercury (autumn) and Saturn (winter).

Regina Angelorum

Billini and Reyes. The nunnery Queen of the Angels is a monumental piece of architecture with huge external buttressing, decaying gargoyles and a sombre stone facade that took nearly a century to build. Knock on the caretaker's door in the back to have a peek inside, where you'll find a Baroque eighteenth-century altar with a stunning silver retable and the marble grave of Padre Francisco Billini at the front of the sanctuary.

Fortaleza Santa Bárbara

Isabela and Puello. Behind the handsome, whitewashed Iglesia Santa Bárbara, are the remains of the Fortaleza Santa Bárbara, to which the church was once attached. Ostensibly part of the city's riverfront defences, the garrison was used mostly to keep the Taino (and later African) slaves in line as they laboured in the nearby limestone quarry – which has long since been paved over and is now the city's downscale shopping district.

▲ MONASTERIO SAN FRANCISCO

The Malecón

Locals descend on the capital's famous oceanfront boardwalk, also known as Avenida George Washington, to kick back and let down their hair. Come evening, the crowds swell with revellers who groove to blaring live music. On New Year's Eve, the Malecón transforms into a waterfront disco, with wild partying and musical entertainment. Dotted along the Malecón's length are a series of outdoor party zones, notably at avenidas Sánchez and Máximo Gómez, and along the commercial port below Puerta San Diego.

The Malecón commences within the colonial district at the large industrial port at the mouth of the Río Ozama. An intact section of the old city wall follows it for 100m to the seventeenth-century San José fort, built on a strategic oceanfront promontory after an attempted invasion by the British in 1655. The cannons that remain appear to point across the street at a fifty-metre-high statue of Fray Montesino, a sixteenth-century priest who preached against the Taino genocide, his legendary rage manifested in the flame-like spikes of his hair.

Gazcue

West of Zona Colonial along the waterfront to Plaza de la Cultura.

The charming, leafy residential district of Gazcue is an inviting base for seeing the capital – in walking distance of both the central sights and the Plaza de la Cultura, but with quiet tree-lined streets and a number of inexpensive hotels dotted throughout.

Museo de Arte Moderno

Plaza de la Cultura ☏685-2154. Tues–Sun 10am–6pm. RD$10.

This excellent museum boasts four storeys dedicated to twentieth-century Dominican art, including works by the highly regarded modern artist Candido Bidó, whose stylized idealizations of campesino life have won international acclaim. Bidó's father was a Carnival mask maker in Bonao – the influence is apparent in the faces with hollowed-out eyes, straight noses and exaggerated lips. The museum owns six Bidós, including his most famous, *El Paseo a las 10am*, a painting of a Dominican woman in a sunhat with a handful of flowers – the pigeon fluttering by her side is a typical Bidó gesture, as is the use of colour: yellow fields, black mountains, indigo sky, and the sun surrounded by a subduing, dark cyst. Also well-known is Silvano Lora's *Flor Endemica*, a mixed-media commentary on the bombed-out urban environment that many of the country's children live in. Lora is an outspoken defender of the oppressed – in 1992, when replicas of Columbus's three ships tried to dock in Santo Domingo in honour of the 500th anniversary of his voyage, Lora dressed up like a Taino, paddled out to the boats in a

▲ SANTO DOMINGO MALECÓN

canoe and fired arrows at them until his vessel was capsized by the Coast Guard.

Museo del Hombre Dominicano

Plaza de la Cultura ☎687-3623. Tues–Sun 10am–5pm. RD$20. The extraordinary Museum of Dominican Man showcases Taino artefacts and a top-notch anthropological exhibit on Dominican fiestas patronales. Head straight to the third floor, which consists of one large room bearing display cases of Taino sculpture, beginning with seated human figures and *cemis* – small stone idols that stood in for the gods during rituals, possessing large, inward-spiralling eyes and flared nostrils. You'll find jewellery with incredibly intricate carvings made from coral, tooth, stone and conch shell, a case filled with spectacularly nasty-looking death's-heads and a few examples of the artwork created by the Tainos' ancestors in the Amazon basin. The fourth floor moves to Dominican culture after Columbus, with emphasis on the African influence, including a terrific exhibit on syncretist religious practices in the DR.

Museo de Historia y Geografía

Plaza de la Cultura ☎686-6668. Tues–Sun 9.30am–4pm. Free. This uneven collection of historical memorabilia from the past two centuries dedicates rooms to the Haitian occupation of the early nineteenth century, the period of internecine strife that followed it, the American occupation that began in 1916 and the thirty-year reign of Trujillo. The American occupation exhibit features

propagandist pamphlets, Marine uniforms and an electric chair in which Dominicans were tortured – above it is a famous photograph of one victim being executed in it, which was used by partisan guerrillas in their efforts to boot the invaders out. The Trujillo-era artefacts testify to the dictator's wealth and absolute power, including gold- and ivory-plated personal effects, his military uniform adorned with dozens of medals and purple presidential sash, and the pancake make-up kit he used to hide his Haitian ancestry. You'll also see the Trujillo portraits and signs offering thanks to "El Benefactor" that were posted in every home and the *cedulas* (identification cards) that citizens were forced to carry with them at all times, identifying them by number. In the centre of the room sits one of the bullet-riddled cars that was part of the presidential motorcade when he was assassinated.

Jardín Botánico

Av Jardín Botánico and Los Próceres ☎385-2611. Daily 9am–6pm. RD$30. The wealthy northern neighbourhood of Arroyo Hondo is home to some of the city's most expansive green spaces, including the botanical gardens, with flora from every part of the island, a pavilion with three hundred types of orchid (most endemic), and greenhouses for bromeliads and aquatic plants. Not indigenous but still quite striking is the manicured Japanese garden with a maze of shrubs and a pagoda with shaded benches beside a babbling brook. An RD$15 train ride will take you through the length of the park with a stop-off at some of the highlights, but

▲ BASEBALL AT ESTADIO QUISQUEYA

it's far more pleasant to wander about the grounds at your leisure.

Museo Prehispánico

San Martín 179 and Lope de Vega. Mon–Fri 9am–5pm. Free. Housed in a large room within the Pepsi-Cola corporate building, the Museo Prehispánico features a private collection of Taino artefacts. A few Venezuelan pieces (the Tainos' ancestral home) provide historical context and serve as a prelude to the fossilized mastodon and armadillo remains, animals the natives hunted to extinction on the island. At the far end of the room you'll see an intact wooden duho – a chair carved with the face of a Taino god, used by caciques as a throne during religious ceremonies.

Estadio Quisqueya

Máximo Gómez and Kennedy ☎542-5772. Tickets RD$50–200. Baseball is the most exciting spectator sport in Santo Domingo; two separate professional teams, Licey and Escogido, play in the winter professional league from mid-November through early February, at Quisqueya Stadium. Tickets are generally available the night of the game, or you can purchase in advance on Wednesday for the weekly

Sunday games – see local newspapers for current ticket-purchasing locations. Though more and more Dominican major-leaguers are opting out of the winter season, you'll still find a few famous Dominican players on the rosters (star Mets hurler Pedro Martínez still pitches for Escogido, for example), along with some of America's top minor-league prospects. The crowds can be quite rowdy, gambling on nearly every event that might soon occur on the field.

Museo Bellapart

Kennedy and Peguero, third floor ☎541-7721. Mon–Fri 10am–6pm, Sat 9am–noon. Free. The small, private Bellapart Museum showcases the best of Dominican art from the first half of the twentieth century. Highlights include social-realist Jaime Colsón's *Merengue*, a surreal rendition of a typical Dominican *fandango* which is strongly influenced by Mexican muralist art; the Deco aesthetic of Celeste Woss y Gill's *Retrato sin fecha*, a lush portrait of a Latin flapper from the Roaring Twenties gracefully scanning a book; and folk artist Yoryi Morel's ragged depiction of a Dominican campo titled *Dedicado a Mi Madre*. The crowning glory of the collection, though, is Spanish exile José Vela Zanetti's *La Vida de los Campesinos* series. The painting here marks a stylistic break from the monumental social-realism of his work on public buildings, sketchier and more attuned to the modernism of Van Gogh, with rough-hewn peasants in front of a whorling, almost formless background of barren rolling hills.

Columbus Lighthouse

℡591-1492. Tues–Sun 9.30am–5.30pm. RD$30. Known locally as El Faro (simply "the lighthouse"), this controversial structure was finally completed, after decades in the making, in 1992 – the 500th anniversary of Columbus's "discovery" of the Americas. The idea for such a tribute dates to the 1850s, and in 1929 an international competition was eventually held for its design. Given that there were over 450 contestants from fifty countries, it's hard to understand how British architect J.C. Gleave's awful, mammoth cross-shaped entry won out; the edifice resembles nothing so much as an immaculately scrubbed penitentiary. Within this bombastic eyesore stands the Baroque mausoleum of Christopher Columbus, though some claim he's not actually buried here. The lighthouse's most impressive feature is the 250-laser cross of light that it projects onto the city's night sky, though even that is resented by many here – it's said that whenever it turns on, power goes out in villages across the country.

Accommodation

Aida

El Conde 474 and Espaillat ℡685-7692. The only hotel with balcony rooms on El Conde and a good bargain for clean, simple accommodation, though the proprietors can be a bit gruff.

It's worth it, though, to sit back on your balcony at night and watch life pass by below you after a long day spent exploring the city. In exchange, you'll have to put up with lukewarm, low-pressure showers. US$34–40.

Conde de Penalba

El Conde 111 and Meriño ℡688-7121, ℗688-7375, ⓦwww.condepenalba.com. A fair compromise between comfort and character, this small hotel tucked away on the second floor of a century-old building on Parque Duarte boasts good service, inviting rooms (a/c, cable TV, phone) and strong hot showers. You pay for the location, though. US$55–75.

Francés

Mercedes 106 and Meriño ℡685-9331, ℗685-1289, ⓦwww.accor-hotels.com. Set in the heart of the colonial district, this beautifully renovated sixteenth-century mansion has nineteen quality private rooms with period furnishings, cable TV, a/c, phone and safe deposit box. The hotel's best feature is its quiet, starlit courtyard. US$100–135.

La Grand Mansión

Danae 26 ℡689-8758. Unpretentious and functional

▲ JAIME COLSÓN PAINTING IN MUSEO BELLAPART

family-run establishment on a quiet residential street, with private hot-water bath, fan, free coffee and nice rooms. Ask for a second-floor room with a view of the trees; a/c for US$2.50 extra. All in all, a terrific value. US$21–27.

Maison Gatreaux

Llúberes 8 ☎687-4856. The large rooms come with a/c, comfortable beds and especially strong hot showers. The rooms are far better than what you'll find in most mid-range hotels in the city and are also quite clean – though the front desk is not especially friendly. US$2 extra for cable TV. US$35–40.

Meliá Santo Domingo

Malecón 365 ☎688-8531, ☎687-4274, ⊛www.solmelia.com. Formerly the *Sheraton*, this luxury establishment boasts a shopping arcade, casino, three restaurants, swimming pool, hot tub and a high-profile disco, though service has gone down a bit. The comfortable rooms come with cable TV, a/c, coffeemaker and phone. US$130–170.

Mercure

El Conde and Hostos ☎688-5500, ☎688-5522, ⊛www.accor-hotels.com. Not as nice as the converted colonial mansions and a bit expensive, but the service is friendly and the rooms are fine in a *Holiday Inn* sort of a way, with all the expected amenities. The breakfast buffet (daily 7–10am) on the ground floor is excellent value and quite popular. US$85–94.

Nicolás de Ovando

Las Damas and El Conde ☎685-9955, ☎686-6590, ⊛www.accor-hotels.com. High-priced luxury hotel in the former home of conquistador

Nicolás de Ovando; spacious rooms blend modern amenities (high-speed Internet connections for one) with an authentic sixteenth-century decor. Half the rooms have great river views, the other half look out on the colonial city – either way, you can't lose. The service is the best around. US$105–165.

Nicolás Nader

Luperón 151 and Duarte ☎687-6674, ☎565-6204, ⊛www.naderenterprises .com/hostal. A well-regarded, small hotel with ten spacious, tastefully decorated rooms in a limestone colonial-era mansion. Within the courtyard are a small art gallery, restaurant and bar. It's a pleasure just to walk through the corridors here, with their ageing, massive limestone blocks lined with portraits of the island's first Spanish nobles. This should be your first mid-range choice in the colonial district. US$50–70.

Palacio

Duarte 106 and Ureña ☎682-4730, ☎687-5535, ⊛www.hotel-palacio .com. If you can't get into the *Nicolás Nader*, this is almost as good – and, unlike its nearby competitor, has free parking. Formerly the residence of infamous *caudillo* Buenaventura Báez, this 1628 mansion has been very well maintained and offers a dozen large, well-appointed rooms, quality service and all the standard amenities. US$70–102.

Renaissance Jaragua

Malecón 367 ☎221-2222, ☎686-0528, ⊛www.marriott.com. This enormous complex is by far the finest of the expensive Malecón resorts. The rooms are big and tastefully appointed and the service is excellent. On the grounds are a popular disco, four restaurants, a bar, swimming pool, hot tub and a tropical garden. For once, you get your money's worth. US$99–160.

Shops

Casa Francia Cigar Shop

Vicioso 103 and Las Damas. This sixteenth-century mansion, home to the French consulate, also has a lobby exhibition that shows the entire process of rolling and growing cigars, with selections of the country's finest cigars for sale at reasonable prices.

Galería Candido Bidó

Dr Báez 5 ☎688-9370. Art gallery set on a residential Gazcue block, run by the most famous of Dominican painters, with a selection of his own work and exhibits from other Dominican modernists like Picasso-influenced Cristian Tiburci, whose massive sculptures of musicians flank the gallery's front door.

Mundo Artesenal

El Conde and Duarte ☎688-3889. Snazzy new jewellery and arts shop where the designers rent stalls within. This makes the quality a bit uneven, with high-end designer jewellery competing for space with somewhat tacky paintings and pottery.

Musicalia

El Conde 464. This renowned bachata record outlet has the best of the Dominican golden oldies, including operatic favourites Eduardo Brito and María Montéz, old bachateros like Luis Segura and *típico* merengueros from Francisco Ulloa to Tavito Vasquez.

Plaza Central

27 de Febrero and Troncoso. Large mall with all the standard shops, including clothing, shoe and CD stores as well as a large cinema.

Thesaurus

Lincoln and Sarasota ⊛www.thesaurus.com.do. Great two-storey bookstore with lots of English-language volumes, and a little espresso café on the second floor.

Restaurants

La Bríciola

Meriño 152 ☎688-5055, ☎www.labriciola.com.do. Impeccable service and elegant, candlelit ambience in a restored colonial palace that features a menu of fresh homemade pastas and seafood. There's also an elegant bar called *Doubles*, where you can order the same food in a more casual environment.

PLACES Santo Domingo

▲ LA BRÍCIOLA

La Cafetera

El Conde 253. Closed Sun. Best of the cafés along El Conde and a hang-out for local painters and musicians. Delicious but greasy traditional Dominican breakfasts with fresh orange juice and café con leche. Also sells the top Dominican rums at great prices, along with cutting-edge Spanish literature.

Costelão

Atarazana 23 ☏688-2773, ⊕www .costelao.com. This new, traditional Brazilian *chiarrascura* has assumed the mantle of best restaurant on Plaza España. The all-you-can-eat 900-peso *riodizio* meals include chicken wings, grilled pork, steak, veal, pork ribs, quail, rabbit, sausage and red snapper. Wash it all down with one of their outstanding *caipirinhas*, which combines fermented sugar-cane juice and lime.

D'Luis Parrillada

Plaza Montesino Malecón and Fiallo. Open 24 hours. The capital's most popular late-night spot, with outdoor seating along the ocean, cheap food and a hyped-up merengue atmosphere. The speciality here is Argentine-style grilled-meat dishes, and the quality of the cooking makes the long waits for service more than worth it.

Don Pepe

Pasteur 41 at Santiago ☏686-8481. If you've budgeted for one big splurge, try *Don Pepe*, old-style high-end Dominican dining at its best. The menu is a display of fresh seafood on ice (try *al horno*-style), including lobster, an assortment of fish and, best of all, giant crab. Don't miss the dessert tray, with its terrific flans, cheesecakes and *crème caramel*.

Look to spend around US$35 per person.

Mesón de Bari

Hostos 302 and Ureña. This local tavern serves great food at affordable prices, particularly the *bistec encebollado* – perhaps the best steak in the country. The exceptionally fresh seafood includes *cangrejos guisados*, a house speciality that features local soft-shell crabs in a garlic sauce. Swift service and fun atmosphere, though it gets rather noisy on weekends when it doubles as an extremely popular local bar and the music is amped up several notches.

Mesón de Luis

Hostos and El Conde, just off Parque Colón. Closed Mon. Run by a friendly local family, this diner serves up breakfasts (the best time to come) and typical Dominican dishes for around RD$90.

La Mezquita

Independencia 407. Outstanding little seafood restaurant with a cozy dining room and a loyal local following. Among the many reasonably priced specialities are *mero* (*criolla* or *al orégano*), octopus and *lambí*.

El Provocón 4to

Santiago and José Pérez, and other locations throughout the city. Open 24 hours. Outdoor patio offering heaping portions of grilled chicken, rice-and-beans and salad. Good for a large, inexpensive lunch.

El Rey de Falafel

Billini 352 and Sánchez. Definitely worth going out of your way for, this popular food stand next to *S Bar* is run by a hip young Israeli-Dominican who makes the freshest, most delicious falafel sandwiches imaginable. Make sure to say "*sin ketchúp*" (without ketchup) or your poor sandwich will pay the consequences.

Samurai
Lincoln 902 and Inchaustegui ☎ 541-0944. No lunch Sun. Authentic Japanese sushi bar, a definite rarity in these parts, with *shabu shabu*, mixed sushi and sashimi platters, hibachi platters and sake. Surprisingly inexpensive considering the high quality.

Vesuvio
Malecón 521 ☎ 221-3333. One of the most renowned restaurants in the city, deservedly so for its vast array of delicious, if expensive, pastas. Particularly recommended are the risotto con frutas del mar and gnocchi gorgonzola.

Bars

Alfatori
Meriño 115. Live acoustic Latin music served up nightly for middle-aged bohemians. Fun ambience and great Italian food as well.

Atarazana 9
Atarazana 9, Plaza España. Super-hip club owned by bachata crooner Juan Luis Guerra, with live music on Thursday nights that favour alternative Latin garage bands.

Café del Teatro
Meriño 110 ☎ 689-3430. Weekend courtyard café in the nineteenth-century Casa del Teatro, a drama venue with live jazz and jazz-influenced Latin combos.

Cubanía
El Conde 53 between Isabela and Las Damas ☎ 333-7001. Don't miss this place – they feature nightly live son from top Cuban musicians in town for the week. Another bonus is the excellent Cuban food such as *ropa vieja*, *bistec encebollado* and black bean shrimp and rice. For drinks, go for the *mojito criollo* which are made with local yerba buena instead of mint. They also have a great collection of Cuban CDs for sale.

La Parada Cerveza
Plaza D'Frank just west of the Hotel Inter-Continental, Malecón. The most popular of the outdoor beer joints dotting the boardwalk and a favourite hang-out of Sammy Sosa. They've recently added a roof and a large neon sign, and are reputed to have the coldest beer in town.

PLACES Santo Domingo

▲ ATARANZA 9

S Bar

Billini and Sánchez. A hip new entry to the crowded field of bars in the Zona Colonial, this place manages to be stylish without putting on any airs. A good place to plug into the scene, and a must on anyone's colonial bar-hopping itinerary.

El Sartín

Hostos 153. An informal place with a rather erratic schedule, so look for the old blue light in front of the building – when the light is on, customers are welcome. It's a fun place to hang out, featuring great Latin hits from yesteryear and a middle-aged crowd of mostly men hanging out and having a good old time.

Clubs and entertainment

La Guácara Taina

Av Mirador del Sur ☎530-0671. Cover RD$100. Probably the most famous club in the city, set in a huge, multi-level natural cave, that now focuses almost exclusively on electronica and is a popular spot for ravers, who call it simply "The Cave".

Jet Set

Independencia 2253 ☎535-4145. Cover RD$75. Very nice, medium-sized seventh-floor disco with great views of the city. Notable because it's so jam-packed with locals every night.

Jubilee

Renaissance Jaragua Hotel, Malecón 367 ☎688-8026. Cover RD$100. Large, luxurious hotel disco featuring top-notch sound and light systems, though drinks are quite expensive.

Mauna Loa

Calle Héroes de Luperón at Malecón, Centro de los Héroes ☎533-2151. Cover RD$60 and one-drink minimum. Super-suave, gorgeous nightclub and casino with two floors of tables looking out onto a big-band stage reminiscent of the Roaring Twenties. Saturday is bolero night with the Francis Santana Orchestra. Sunday nights are even better: son night with Chichi y los Soneros de Haina. The club opens at 6pm, but the music doesn't start until 11pm.

Monumento del Son

Av Charles de Gaulle and Los Restauradores, Sabana Perdida, east of the Río Ozama and 5km north of Las Américas Highway ☎590-3666. Cover RD$50. Famous outdoor son hall set in a safe neighbourhood, with live music Fri–Mon. Features a lot of corny old vaudeville stuff, including an emcee ventriloquist with a puppet. Don't miss this place – it's the ultimate Santo Domingo son experience.

▲ SON PERFORMERS

The Southeast

The Southeast's beautiful sandy beaches, peppered with all-inclusive resorts, generally draw travellers looking for a comfortable Caribbean experience with food and drinks included in the hotel price tag. There are, however, plenty of opportunities to explore vast tracts of remote mangrove swamp, go sportfishing, discover historic ruins like Ponce de León's home and hike through a cave system that holds a plethora of Taino rock art. The ever-growing resorts – including the world's most massive at Punta Cana/Bávaro and the smaller enclaves of Bayahibe, Boca Chica and Juan Dolio – sprawl alongside mid-sized industrial cities that once served as centres for sugar processing. The further east you go, the more beautiful the beach and the less there is to do outside your hotel walls – the gorgeous twenty-kilometre-plus strand of soft white sand along Playa Punta Cana simply has to be seen to be believed.

Boca Chica

25km east of Santo Domingo. Boca Chica curves along a small bay protected by shoals, with wonderfully transparent Caribbean water paralleling a long line of beach shacks serving excellent food. It used to be one of the island's prime swimming spots, but the town that surrounds it has unfortunately become so crowded with freelance guides, sex workers and persistent touts that it's impossible to walk more than a few feet without being accosted by some enterprising individual hell-bent on attaching themselves to you for the duration of your stay. On the weekends, the beach is jam-packed with thousands of day-tripping city-dwellers swimming in the sea and dancing to a cacophony of car stereos – an unforgettable beach-party scene. At night, after the Dominicans leave, it becomes little more than a gringo brothel. Sitting on the

Getting there and getting around

If you're in the majority of travellers who come to the Southeast as part of a package tour, you'll be flying into one of the international airports at Punta Cana, La Romana or Santo Domingo. Your hotel should provide free airport pickup, so make sure they're apprised of your arrival time and look for their touts at the airport exit. None of the major national bus companies provides regular service to the region, which means independent travellers will either have to rent a car (the most convenient option) or make do with the local, second-tier mini-van and guagua operators that ferry locals from one town to another. There's a thrice-daily express bus from Santo Domingo's Parque Enriquillo to Punta Cana; most other trips to Bávaro and Punta Cana involve at least a stopover in Higüey with a somewhat long hike to the separate, eastbound guagua station.

beach is the main attraction, and the waters are low and calm enough to walk out to the bird-inhabited mangrove island La Matica just off shore.

Juan Dolio

45km east of Boca Chica. The twenty-five-kilometre-long line of rocky coast between Boca Chica and San Pedro de Macorís holds a strip of vacation homes and all-inclusives collectively

known as Juan Dolio. Though popular, this package resort area has never quite matched its rivals, mainly because of the beach; the sand is perfectly acceptable but the expanse of dead coral under the water makes swimming and walking in the water uncomfortable, and the private hotel beaches are quite small – simply no match for what you'll find further east at Punta Cana and Bávaro.

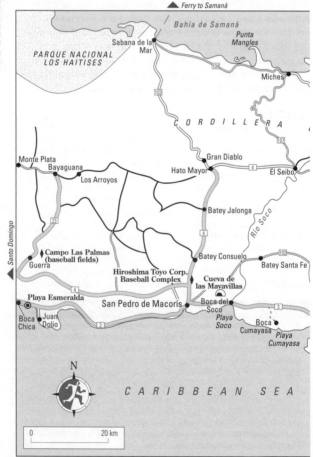

That said, Juan Dolio does have a few advantages over its regional competitors: there's none of the large-scale harassment of Boca Chica, and, unlike Bávaro, you'll find a number of quality restaurants and budget hotels geared towards independent travellers. Also, the nightlife is good, and you're still within shouting distance of Santo Domingo. The main drag, at Villas del Mar,

▲ JUAN DOLIO BAR

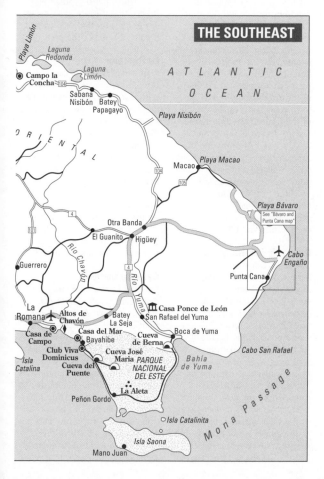

THE SOUTHEAST

is lined with hotels, Internet kiosks, souvenir shops and the like.

San Pedro de Macorís

70km east of Santo Domingo. This crowded city owes its uneven development to the boom-and-bust fortunes of the sugar industry. Victorian civic monuments built during the crop's glory years stand along the eastern bank of the Río Higuamo, a far cry from the squalor of the surrounding neighbourhoods and the shut gates at more than half of the area's seven mills. What redeems it is the Malecón, a wide seaside boardwalk with modest public beaches at either end, celebrated by bachata star Juan Luis Guerra in his song *Guavaberry*: "I like to sing my song/in the middle of the Malecón/watching the sun go down/in San Pedro de Macorís". At night and on weekends, it's quite the buzzing scene – sharp-dressed locals pour onto the promenade or just linger on the concrete benches that line it, while vendors hawk fast food, boiled corn, candy and Clorets.

Cueva de las Maravillas

5km east of San Pedro de Macorís on Highway 3 ☎696-1797, www .cuevadelasmaravillas.com. Tues–Sun 10am–6pm. RD$100 adults, RD$50 children under 12. These first-rate caves boast scores of Taino petroglyphs, beautifully odd geologic formations, and walkways with motion-sensor lighting that ease exploration during the one-hour guided tours. There are also ramps for wheelchair access to many areas of the cave system. Only a few of the guides speak English, but they're well-versed in the cave's history and the significance of

▲ ALTOS DE CHAVÓN

the various petroglyphs. For RD$100 you can purchase a set of booklets on the rock art and flora and fauna of the cave.

La Romana

37km east of San Pedro. La Romana is a workaday town with not much to offer travellers aside from a glimpse into daily Dominican life and a lively night-time scene. A walk along the rambling pastel barrio that borders the river's western bank makes for a pleasant hour. The Parque Central is the major meeting place, and from its northwestern corner sprawls an outdoor market that stretches north for several blocks, chock-full of fresh produce, household wares and cheap knick-knacks.

Casa de Campo

East of La Romana off Highway 4 ☎523-3333, ☎523-8548, ☺www .casadcampo.com. A huge resort built by Gulf & Western in the 1970s, Casa de Campo is really a sight unto itself, and worth a visit even if you're not staying there. The complex encompasses seven thousand meticulously manicured acres of rolling hills set along the sea and boasts two golf courses – including Pete Dye's famous "Teeth of the Dog", with eight of its holes right along the oceanfront – a

24-hour tennis centre, fourteen swimming pools, equestrian stables with horseback riding and polo grounds, a sporting clay course, personal trainers, a beauty spa and so forth. In addition to the spacious, comfortable rooms, there are 150 luxury private villas with butler, private chef and maid, used by (among others) Madonna, Elizabeth Taylor and former US presidents Jimmy Carter and Bill Clinton. If you're staying here, you're best off renting a car (which can be done at the resort or from the airport), as the system of shuttle buses that ferry visitors back and forth across the resort are notoriously slow.

The crowning pleasure is **Playa Minitas**, a gorgeous strand of beach protected by a shallow coral reef – nice enough that some spend their whole vacation on it; it's not technically open to the public, but you won't be questioned unless you ask for a towel. Just as nice is nearby **Isla Catalina**, a small island 2km off shore reachable by shuttle boats, where *Casa de Campo* has set up a small dock, a few pavilions and a shaded restaurant/bar. Several local tours and cruise ships drop anchor just off the island and ferry thousands of passengers back and forth via speedboats, so expect big crowds.

Altos de Chavón

2km east of Casa de Campo. A high-concept shopping mall perched atop a cliff overlooking the Río Chavón, Altos de Chavón was constructed to the specifications of a sixteenth-century Italian village with artificially aged limestone. Though its cobblestone streets are littered with double-parked tour buses and its "Tuscan" villas crammed to the gills with dimestore souvenirs, it's still a pleasant place to spend an afternoon. The 5000-seat open-air amphitheatre is undeniably impressive and the small **archeology museum** (daily 9.30am–5pm; free; ☎682-3111) is quite excellent, with a variety of Taino artefacts, including two intact canoes and a wooden *cahoba* idol culled from Parque Nacional del Este.

Bayahibe

20km east of La Romana. Sitting right on the ocean, Bayahibe boasts a dozen cheap, clean cabañas run by local families, making it a relaxed spot for independent travellers to stay for a couple of nights. You'll also find several mom-and-pop waterfront restaurants where you can enjoy tasty, inexpensive meals. If you fancy something more luxurious, there are several all-inclusive resorts just east of town, set along one of the most

▼ BAYAHIBE

dramatic beaches on the entire island. Bayahibe is also the best base from which to explore the beaches and caves of nearby Parque Nacional del Este.

Parque Nacional del Este

Park is best accessed on boat tours (RD$75) offered through local hotels; tours depart from park entrance at Bayahibe. This expansive national park takes in a maze of forests, trails, caves and cliffs that flourish with birdlife, along with Isla Saona. Not much of it, however, is conveniently accessible; in fact, no roads lead directly into its interior, and the best method of approach is to hire boats from Bayahibe to hit specific points along the rim, from where you can hike inland. Wherever you go in the park, wear plenty of mosquito repellent, as wasps are fairly prevalent here. Watch out, too, for tarantulas, though they won't bother you unless they're antagonized.

The most popular section – and rightfully so – is **Isla Saona**, an island off the southern coast lined with alternating stretches of idyllic, coconut-tree-backed beachfront and mangrove swamp, unpopulated except for two fishing hamlets. That said, the traffic at Saona has increased exponentially in recent years,

and despite its reputation as a pristine natural oasis, the most popular stopoff points for boat tours have begun to feel more like high season at Miami's South Beach. The largest ships pull in to Isla Saona at **Mano Juan**, a strip of pastel shacks with a four-kilometre hiking trail leading inland, or **Piscina Natural** (known locally as Laguna Canto de la Playa), a sand bar backed by a clear lagoon where you can splash about. Boats can also be hired to **Peñon Gordo** on the national park's west coast (2hr each way), which has a little isolated beach of its own, as well as a large cave 2km inland that's good for exploring.

Boca de Yuma

45km east of Bayahibe. Though lacking a spectacular beachfront, Boca de Yuma does have a fairly nice strip of sand across the Río Yuma and a new clifftop park in the centre of town. The pueblo's setting along squat, ocean-pounded bluffs is undeniably impressive and makes a pleasant stop for those seeking relaxation away from the resort zones – though there are no hotels in town, so you'll have to visit on a day-trip. Boca de Yuma is also one of the best spots to fish for marlin in the entire Caribbean, and it's a good entry point to many of the sights in the Parque Nacional del Este.

Within the tiny town you can wander along the shore, which has several surf-crashing grooves cut into the rock, or pay a local fisherman

▲ ISLA SAONA

RD$20 to ferry you across the Río Yuma to a pretty little beach called **Playa Borinquen** that you'll share only with a couple of grazing cows. A short walk west of town along the waterfront is the national park station at the eastern entrance to Parque Nacional del Este, from where you can hire horses or walk for an hour along the water to a natural land bridge where turbulent jets of sea water rocket into the air. Near the station is the cavernous **Cueva de Berna**, a large cave once inhabited by Tainos. Along with hundreds of bats and small birds, you'll see Taino *caritas* (little faces) carved on the walls, though some have been defaced by graffiti.

Casa Ponce de León

Northwest of Boca de Yuma, San Rafael de Yuma. Mon–Sat 9am–5pm. RD$30. The fortified Casa Ponce de León was the remote medieval keep built by Taino slaves for the noted explorer, who established a working farm and sugar plantation here during his rule of nearby Higüey at the beginning of the sixteenth century. Ponce didn't stay here for long, however; in 1508 he increased his holdings by setting up a slave-catching outpost in Puerto Rico, which quickly grew into a colony in its own right, proving more profitable than his Dominican estate. Following this venture he set off for Florida, where he died at the hands of natives while searching for the Fountain of Youth. Inside the house, you'll get a guided tour of a museum with exhibits meant to evoke de León's life and times, including original mahogany furnishings, along with de León's suit of armour and bulky treasure chest.

Higüey

45km northeast of Bayahibe. Cramped, dusty and one hundred percent concrete, Higüey is an unpleasant town of 150,000 that's worth knowing about mainly because you may have to pass through on your way to the east coast beaches. It is also a place of pilgrimage: tens of thousands gather here each January 21 for a mammoth procession and prayer of intercession to the nation's patron saint, the Virgin of Altagracia. They head to the modernist **Basílica de Nuestra Señora de la Merced**, whose eighty-metre arch is visible from the entire city, and actually most impressive when viewed from a distance, as the grounds around it are garbage-strewn.

Punta Cana and Bávaro

35km east of Higüey. The tropical playlands of Punta Cana and Bávaro sprawl on either end of a long curve of coconut-tree-lined beach. Go elsewhere if you want to explore the country: the individual resorts tend to be cities unto themselves, encompassing vast swaths of beachside territory, expansive tropical gardens and several separate hotels. Fortunately, the beach is big enough that it doesn't get overly crowded despite the 750,000 visitors each year; with enough fortitude you could walk some 30km without seeing the sand interrupted once. At points where resorts have cropped up, you'll find the requisite concentration of beach umbrellas, watersports outfitters and bars, with occasional souvenir shacks set up in between. Aside from the glass-bottom boat operators trying to drum up business, though, there's relatively little hassle

The Southeast PLACES

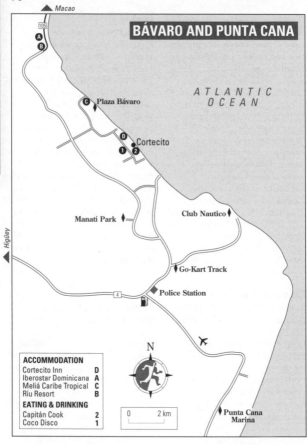

▲ Macao

BÁVARO AND PUNTA CANA

ATLANTIC OCEAN

Ⓐ
Ⓑ

Ⓒ Plaza Bávaro

Ⓓ Cortecito
❶❷

▲ Higüey

Manatí Park

Club Nautico

Go-Kart Track

Police Station

N

▼ Punta Cana Marina

ACCOMMODATION
Cortecito Inn   D
Iberostar Dominicana A
Meliá Caribe Tropical C
Ríu Resort   B

EATING & DRINKING
Capitán Cook   2
Coco Disco   1

0   2 km

– and the all-inclusives here are the nicest on the island.

Cortecito

Playa Bávaro, 15km north of Punta Cana. The only village left along a resort-dominated stretch, Cortecito is an agreeable hang-out populated by backpackers, independent European vacationers and a slew of Dominican vendors, with souvenir stalls set up along the public-access beach. Many congregate around the beach-volleyball net at the north end

of town, and there are often bonfire beach parties here at night. Away from the water, activity slows down quite a bit and the landscape becomes rather bleak. One option is the Tropical Racing go-kart track at the turnoff that separates upper and lower Bávaro (daily 4–10pm; US$15 for 25min; ☎707-5164, Ⓦwww .tropicalracing.com), most exciting when it's crowded with daredevil Dominican teenagers taking the corners too fast.

Macao

9km north of Bávaro. With its pounding surf that has warded off hotel chains and many would-be vacationers, Macao feels refreshingly remote. No paved roads approach it; look instead for a rusty sign that points to the sand road that leads to Macao from just north of the *Ríu Resort*. You're best off swimming at Macao's southern cove, which is framed by majestic bluffs that themselves make for a diverting hour's hike. The only nearby building is the downscale *Cabañas/Restaurant* (no phone; RD$200), with modest accommodation (cold-water bath, fan and not much else) and a mediocre lunch.

Laguna Redondo

20km northwest of Varma on Highway 104. Protected as a national park, Laguna Redondo is of interest mostly to serious birdwatchers. It's especially difficult to reach – though a rusted sign points to the turnoff, you can only get to its banks with a 4WD. There are no boats dedicated to travellers out, though occasionally a fishing boat nearby can be enticed to do the job for RD$100. Even if you're stuck on shore, you'll see a number of birds, including the predatory osprey, egrets, horneate spoonbills and herons.

Laguna Limón

24km north of Varma on Highway 104. More accessible than Laguna Redondo is the beautiful and serene Laguna Limón (also part of the national park), with a couple of small outfits around

it dedicated to tourism. Two separate entrances lead to it from the highway, the first of which is marked by a small national park station (9.30am–noon & 2–5pm; RD$30), where a local guide with a boat can be hired (RD$700 for three to four people). The second entrance is 2km further west; there's no park station here, so you won't be asked to pay the fee. Another 2km on stands *La Cueva* (☎689-4664; reservations necessary), a restaurant with fresh seafood and lobster that caters mostly to passing tour buses on their way to Los Haitises and guests of the nearby hotel. They can also arrange boat trips to the lagoon if given one day's notice, and with less hassle and confusion than you'll have to put up with at the park office.

A hundred metres further on, the road veers right at **Playa Limón**, another of the spectacular area beaches, though the undertow is strong enough to preclude swimming and it's plagued by sand fleas at dusk. It does, though, make for a scenic walk, and sea turtles lay their eggs here in the spring.

Costa Esmeralda

15km northwest of Laguna Limón and east of Miches. Gorgeous Costa

▼ PLAYA EL LIMÓN

Esmeralda boasts a series of sandy beaches that extend for several kilometres. Enter from Playa Miches, via a marked dirt path directly across the Río Miches from town. You can either walk, drive or arrange for a horseback ride at your hotel for around US$20. The sand extends for 8km, though there are a couple of small rivers to ford. You can also get local fishers to take you out to Media Luna, a half-moon of sand that peeks out of the ocean at low tide, several kilometres offshore. Trips will generally cost around RD$200; make sure yourself that the ship is sturdy, and it's advised that women not go out alone in a local boat.

Parque Nacional Los Haitises

Book an organized tour with your hotel or hire a guide at the national park office (☏556-7333) at the port on the east end of Sabana de la Mar; guided tours start at RD$2700 for up to six people, plus RD$50 park fee. This massive expanse of mangrove swamp protects several Taino caves, 92 plant species, 112 bird species and a wide variety of marine life. Along the coast it holds the country's largest unblemished stretch of red and white mangroves. Only a small portion of its twelve hundred square kilometres is open to the public, and what you'll see on boat tours is a series of virtually untouched mangrove rivers along with small islands and coastal caves that provide habitat for untold numbers of tropical birds. Some of the caves, too, bear Taino petroglyphs.

Accommodation

Campo la Concha

Playa Esmeralda, Sabana Miches ☏248-5884. Six basic cabañas, well maintained with fan and shared cold-water bath, a library full of eclectic books and CDs and a nice little restaurant, all of it way out in the middle of nowhere on a superb beach that you'll have all to yourself. Come here if you want simplicity, serenity and natural beauty – and don't mind staying rooted in one place for the duration of your stay. The proprietor also owns a couple of well-groomed horses for rides along the beach. US$35–45.

Casa de Campo

Highway 3, 2km west of La Romana ☏523-3333, ☏523-8548, ☏www .casadcampo.com. This place will not disappoint: the rooms are large, well appointed and include all the amenities one would expect for the price. Decor is more in line with top-flight corporate hotels, as opposed to the dreary motel rooms you'll find in most Dominican all-inclusives. There are also expensive private cottages which can cost as much as US$1500 a night. US$100–140.

▼ FISHING BOATS NEAR MICHES

Casa del Mar

West of Bayahibe ⊕221-8880, ⑰221-8881. Lush resort set apart from the others, which makes the beach much less crowded. The all-turquoise grounds hold the usual array of services and amenities, including three restaurants (the Thai-oriented one is best), a disco, horseback excursions, a beach bar and an amazing pool area. Most of the comfortable rooms offer ocean views. US$95–130.

Club Viva Dominicus

East of Bayahibe ⊕686-5658, ⑰221-6806, ⑯www.vivaresorts.com. The first of the all-inclusives to be built in this area, and still one of the best. A lavish compound frequented mostly by Italian tourists that offers good food, a great beach, numerous watersports, tennis, aerobics and a dive centre. You can choose between a standard a/c hotel room and a more primitive but private bungalow. US$125 for rooms, and US$150 for bungalows.

Coco Loco

Playa Miches, Miches ⊕553-5920, ⑰553-5839, ⑯www.abatrex.com/cocoloco. Located just across the river from town on pretty Playa Miches, this small independent hotel boasts simple but genuinely comfortable private cabañas with hot-water showers; there's also a small restaurant on site that serves out-of-this-world breakfasts, including fresh fruit shakes. The best thing about the place is the location, along a stretch of scenic beach that sees little traffic. US$30–40.

Cortecito Inn

Calle Playa Cortecito, Bávaro ⊕552-0639, ⑰552-0641. If you don't want to go all-inclusive, this is the place for you in Bávaro. It's right by the beach in the heart of Cortecito village, and has better accommodation than the larger resorts. Some rooms have private balconies, and there's also a swimming pool and restaurant. Breakfast included. US$55–75.

Europa

Dominguez and Duarte, Boca Chica ⊕523-5721, ⑰523-6994, ⑯htleuropa@verizon.net.do. Highly recommended French-run hotel right on the beach with sociable and efficient proprietors who keep the place up to the highest standards and make everybody feel at home. The 33 comfortable rooms (five with sea view) have king-sized beds, but beyond that each is uniquely decorated. There's one three-bedroom for large groups, and several cheap economy rooms. US$40–65.

Fior di Loto

Calle Principal 51, Juan Dolio ⊕526-1146, ⑰526-3332, ⑯hfdiloto@verizon.net.do. The most appealing hotel in Juan Dolio by a long shot, and a major hang-out for independent travellers. The India-themed rooms are simple but comfortable and fun, with visitors adding to the ornate Far Eastern patterns painted on the walls – which are based on the lattice-work of a palace in Rajasthan. All rooms have hot water, cable TV and fan; some also offer kitchenettes. In addition to the usual hotel amenities, they host yoga, meditation, martial arts and massage sessions – plus there's a large gym, a hot tub, a very private sun deck and a small multi-faith chapel. A fun and relaxing place to stay. US$20–50.

Howard Johnson Macorix

Malecón and Deligne, San Pedro de

Macorís ☎529-2100, ⓕ529-9239, ⓔhj.macorix@verizon .net.do. Surprisingly high-quality business hotel in the heart of San Pedro. Quiet, comfortable rooms with balconies, impeccable service, and a swimming-pool area that thrums with live merengue on weekends. US$45–65.

Iberostar Dominicana Hotel

Playa Bávaro ☎221-6500, ⓕ688-9888 or 221-1552, ⓦwww.iberostar .com. Enormous complex with huge rooms, good service and an attractive beachfront area – perfect for an all-inclusive vacation, provided you don't mind the mediocre food. Get up early to reserve a seat at the steakhouse for dinner, the best restaurant on the complex. There's also a spa with hot tubs (though you have to pay extra for it) and a casino. Most guests here do not speak English, so picking up a bit of Spanish beforehand will hold you in good stead with the staff. US$100–175.

Meliá Caribe Tropical

Playa Bávaro ☎686-7499, ⓕ686-7699, ⓦwww.solmelia.com. The top Bávaro resort, slightly more expensive but well worth it, with opulent contemporary architecture, sculpted tropical gardens, and the option of suites or bungalows. Luxurious amenities include bathrobes, a daily newspaper of your choice and a glass of champagne upon arrival. Sporting options abound, from volleyball, water polo and beach soccer to horseback riding and tennis, plus there's a large gym and a dive shop. *Waterfront Licey* is the best of the restaurants. US$130–180.

Playa Esmeralda

Carretera Las Américas Km 36, Juan Dolio ☎526-3434, ⓕ526-1744, ⓦwww.hotel-playaesmeralda.com. Lovely, quiet hotel way off the main Juan Dolio strip, and closer to the village of Guayacanes. The beach here is far better than what you'll find in the main resort zone (with plenty of good snorkelling), the private grounds swarm with songbirds and the spacious rooms have all the usual amenities. US$50–70.

Ríu Resort

Playa Bávaro ☎221-7171, ⓕ682-1645, ⓦwww.riu.com. Classy Julio Iglesias brainchild with swimming pools punctuated by artificial palm islands. Great food and service, and some rooms come with a private hot tub. Extras include a casino, tennis courts, dive school, windsurfing and deep-sea fishing. The Taino, Naiboa and Melao compounds are all-inclusive, but the pricier Palace is not, and features more luxury amenities like in-room Jacuzzi and room service. Melao's *La Proa* restaurant is particularly good. All-inclusive starts at US$120; the Palace, $150–200, depending on the view.

Villa Iguana

Bayahibe ☎833-0203, ⓦwww .villaiguana.de. A small guest house run by the local dive shop with clean, modest rooms (some with a/c) and a spacious apartment. You also get free breakfast, pickup from La Romana airport and a bicycle that you can use for free. US$30–40.

Zapata

Abraham Núñez 27, Boca Chica ☎523-4777, ⓕ523-5534, ⓔg.zapata@verizon.net.do. If you find yourself staying in Boca Chica, try out this hotel, with a

▲ MELIÁ CARIBE TROPICAL

huge, secluded beachfront bar, doorman, strong showers and free breakfast if you're staying two nights or more. US$35–50.

Restaurants

Boca Marina

Prolongación Duarte 12, Boca Chica ☎523-6702. Fantastic seafood that's relatively pricey at around RD$500 per meal, but well worth it. Try the red snapper or dorado filet, or go for heaping plates of grilled shrimp, ceviche and fried *calamari*. The waterfront setting is also ideal; if you bring your bathing suit, you can jump off the edge of the restaurant and swim between courses. Also the best service in town.

Boca Yate

Playa Bayahibe, west of Bayahibe village along the strip of all-inclusive resorts. Small independent restaurant/hotel delivers with authentic, high-quality Italian fare, including an array of excellent pastas and grilled fish at a reasonable RD$200 per plate. Specialities include penne with lobster tail and a kingfish filet in mushroom sauce.

Capitán Cook

Playa Cortecito, Bávaro ☎552-1061. Great, tourist-oriented seafood palace with tables set up right on the sand. The massive circular charcoal grill is always packed with whole red snapper, lobster, shrimp, *calamari* and conch. Budget for around RD$500 per person.

Comedor

Calle Segunda, Bayahibe. An unmarked food shack with delicious *pollo al carbón* (with *wasakaka*, whatever that is) as well as fresh fried fish, tostones, beans and rice – depending on what the chef cooks that day. It's traditional to wash it down with a shot of rum or a swig of the local Dominican moonshine.

Deli Suisse

Calle Duarte at the beach, Guayacanes. A rather modest-looking fish eatery in a village just west of Juan Dolio, with grilled fish guaranteed to have come out of the ocean that very day. Not super-cheap and with somewhat slow service, but the food is worth it.

▲ BOCA YATE

Neptuno

Prolongación Duarte 8, Boca Chica ☎523-4703. Popular formal gourmet seafood restaurant with lovely views of the ocean. Terrific mixed seafood platters, lobster ravioli and prawns for around RD$650 per person. Reservations are a good idea on weekends.

El Pescador

Casa de Campo. An outdoor patio set up right on the beach with an array of excellent seafood dishes. The accent here is on Cajun spices, with blackened sea bass, creole langostinas and a superb shellfish *bouillabaisse*. The combination of ambience and quality seafood is hard to top.

Restaurant El Sueño

Calle Principal 330, Juan Dolio ☎526-3903. The most elegant Juan Dolio restaurant, and a bit more expensive than its competitors, this impeccable little spot is set on an outdoor patio with white linen tablecloths and impeccable service. Try the chicken scaloppini in white wine sauce, filet of bass in mushroom sauce or grilled dorado.

Robby Mar

Av Charro, San Pedro de Macorís ☎529-4926. A superb seafood restaurant in San Pedro, across the street from the cathedral. Given that it's tucked away behind the brightly coloured stalls where fishermen sell the day's catch to city residents, the restaurant has a remarkably romantic ambience, with candlelit outdoor tables that look out on the river. The prices are reasonable, and every menu item is worth trying, including the shrimp, lobster and grilled fish.

Shish Kabab

Marquez 32, La Romana. An excellent little Lebanese kitchen just off La Romana's Parque Central, with festive indoor/outdoor seating and delicious chicken skewers, hummus platters, falafel and out-of-this-world baklava.

Bars

Café Giulia

Villas del Mar 288, Juan Dolio. This casual little bar is a major local hang-out. Also has a small dancing area with mostly American music and some merengue thrown in here and there.

Chocolate Bar

Calle Central 127, Juan Dolio. Outdoor bar fronting a local strip mall, with a pool table and big crowds on weekends. Simple, but the most popular spot in town to chill out after a day on the beach.

Freedom

Villas del Mar 320, Juan Dolio. Enjoy tasty pub grub and real pints at this British-run sports pub that's a focal point for the expat community and a great place to get to know the area. In addition to covering all the major sporting events from across the world, they have theme-night dinners during the week – including excellent Indian curries on Thursday night.

Ketty Berard

Calle Segunda, Bayahibe. A pleasantly low-key hang-out housed in a thatched hut that features ice-cold beer, local rum drinks and tasty Haitian food. You can expect to meet a good number of locals here.

Pequeña Suiza

Calle Duarte, Boca Chica. Popular outdoor bar on Boca Chica's main strip that features the usual assortment of alcoholic drinks plus cappuccinos and decent bar food. Great spot to sit back and watch the inevitable Boca Chica chaos.

Subway

Av Independencia at Plaza 30/30, San Pedro de Macorís. Super-popular bar and dance hall owned by baseball star Sammy Sosa. The music is mostly techno and house, and the crowds are composed entirely of locals. Overall an interesting experience, but with a bit too much of a Latin machismo vibe for some visitors.

Clubs and entertainment

7-14

27 de Febrero, San Pedro de Macorís. Cover RD$40. Popular local nightclub that features great all-bachata sets on Friday afternoons and evenings. You won't be encountering many other foreigners here – this place is 100 percent Dominican and proud of it.

El Batey

Calle Principal 84, Juan Dolio. Juan Dolio's one disco, with a mixed crowd of locals and tourists. Come on Saturdays, when the place is jam-packed and a lot of fun. The rest of the week it's only moderately populated.

Coco Disco

At entrance to Cortecito. Cover RD$100. This place looks like a traditional rural Dominican dance hall complete with thatch roof but pulls in a huge crowd from the surrounding resorts. A little seedy, but they do occasionally feature major live acts like Raulín Rodríguez and Los Hermanos Rosario.

Genesis

Altos de Chavón. Open Thurs–Sat. Cover RD$150. Weekend getaway for wealthy kids from Santo Domingo who've come to Casa de Campo for a break from city life. Look for a big dose of heavy-handed hip-hop, Euro-electronica and designer clothes, plus a line of Mercedes Benzes in the parking lot.

Lexus

Malecón, San Pedro de Macorís. Popular two-tiered San Pedro dance hall on the waterfront. A totally crowded madhouse that tops off a night cruising the city's seaside boardwalk.

Ricamo

Calle Gonzalvo, off Parque Central, La Romana. Cover RD$40. Come here to see how the Dominicans do it down in the barrios. A fairly nice place where sharp dress is required and people don't really start showing up until midnight.

Samaná Peninsula

The most appealing part of the entire country, the Samaná Peninsula features a beautiful coast lined with spectacular beaches that conform strictly to the Caribbean archetype of powdery white sand, vast banks of swaying coconut trees and transparent green-blue sea. The beach towns of Las Terrenas and Las Galeras serve as popular hubs for independent tourism while away

from the water looms the Cordillera Samaná, an imposing mountain range thick with sixty different types of palm tree and a series of spectacular waterfalls. Perhaps even more than the lovely beaches and geography, visitors come to the peninsula to view up close the thousands of humpback whales that migrate to the Bahía de Samaná during the winter.

▲ SAMANÁ MALECÓN

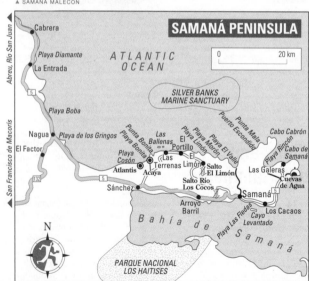

Getting there and getting around

There are two small airports on the Samaná Peninsula, with another slated to open in 2006, but the vast majority who come here fly into Puerto Plata and travel east along the Carretera 5. In mid-2006, a new superhighway is meant to cut the travel time between Samaná and Santo Domingo's Las Américas airport to two hours by car. Public transport to the city of Samaná is straightforward, with both Caribe Tours and Metro running regular bus service here from Puerto Plata, Santiago and Santo Domingo. Getting out to Las Galeras or Las Terrenas means taking a guagua. If you're already in Samaná, you're best off taking the newly paved highway that links the city with both El Limón and Las Terrenas. Guaguas also depart from the Samaná Malecón to Las Galeras hourly during the daytime.

Samaná

Protected on its southern side by an elongated strip of land that breaks apart into a series of small islands, Santa Bárbara de Samaná possesses a remarkably safe and attractive harbour. A flotilla of sailboats stands behind the palm-ridged island chain, and the port and wide-open promenade bordering the water hustle with activity. Most travellers use Samaná as a base to **whale watch** and explore the area beaches, returning in the evening to enjoy the lively nightlife along the broad **Malecón**, packed with outdoor cafés, shops and patches of park. At the Samaná harbour's western promontory begins the so-called Bridge to Nowhere, linking the town to Cayo Linares and Cayo Vigia. Just west of the whitewashed, now defunct *Cayacoa Resort* lies the small city beach, **Playa Escondido**.

La Churcha

Santa Bárbara and Duarte, Samaná. Daily 9am–6pm. The old First African Wesleyan Methodist Church of Samaná, a prefabricated, tin-roofed structure popularly known as La Churcha, was originally shipped over by the English Methodist Church in 1823, to support the African-Americans who

emigrated here during Haitian rule in 1824–25. Most of these were freed slaves, who for the most part managed to maintain their culture despite sustained persecution by Trujillo and a subsequent lack of interest in younger generations carrying on the traditions. One ongoing custom is the series of yearly **harvest festivals**, community feasts with African-American church music held every Friday from late August to the end of October. The celebrated festival is in a different church in the neighbouring countryside every week, culminating in the final festival at La Churcha.

▲ LA CHURCHA

Las Galeras & A ▲

SAMANÁ

African
Methodist
Church

See inset map

MALECÓN

B

AV. ROSARIO SÁNCHEZ

Sánchez (32km)

American
Express
El Mercado

2

C

1

N

0   300 m

Cayo
Linares   BRIDGE TO NOWHERE

Cayo Vigia

Playa
Escondido

Bahía de Samaná

ACCOMMODATION	
Bahía View	C
Gran Bahía	A
Tropical Lodge	B
EATING & DRINKING	
Cachet	2
Café de Paris	5
Don Juan	B
Le France	4
Naomi	3
Plaza Mimi	1

La Churcha

DOWNTOWN

0   50 m

CALLE SANTA BARBARA

Pharmacy

Port
Authority

Laundromat

Caribe Tours
(Bus
Station)

Bandstand

Metro
Bus
Station

Verizon/
Western
Union

Las Olas

Xamana Car/
Bike Rental

3
465

Samaná
Tourist Service

MALECÓN

Banco
Popular

@

Victoria
Marine/
Whale
Samaná

Port

Cayo Levantado

US$20 ferry from Samaná's main port.
Cayo Levantado is the original
Bacardi Island photographed
in the 1970s rum campaign,
though the particular swaying
palm from the ad has since been
uprooted in a tropical

storm; fortunately, hundreds of
others still line the white sands.
The resort hotel that once
dominated the island is currently
closed but ferries still drop off
hundreds of day-trippers, so
be prepared for crowds at the
main beach. It's possible to find
a bit more
solitude by
following the
path extending
inland across
the island to
the smaller
beaches on
the opposite
side. But
with constant
hassling from

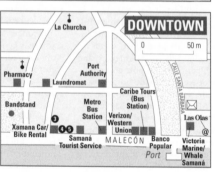

▲ CAYO LEVANTADO

vendors and extortionate food and drink prices across the island, it's definitely a case of paradise ruined and, unless you're visiting as part of a whale-watching tour, there are many better places on the peninsula to spend a day

▲ HORSERIDING ON LAS GALERAS BEACH

on the beach. At night, Cayo Levantado sees much less traffic, and you can camp on the more remote side – though you'll need permission from the port officials first, which will cost you RD$100. You can ask them directly at the Samaná port, but your best bet is to go through Victoria Marine (☎ & ℱ 538-2494).

Las Galeras

25km east of Samaná. Set in a horseshoe-shaped cove at the eastern end of the peninsula, this sleepy outpost has seen considerable changes over the last few years, including the construction of *Casa Marina Bay*, a large all-inclusive resort just east of town, and numerous

other hotels near the main beach entrance. Despite this, the small village has managed to maintain its peaceful and timeless ambience. It may no longer be the undiscovered gem it was only a few years ago, but the sweeping curve of pure white sand, upon which an almost unbelievably turquoise sea laps gently, remains as beautiful as ever.

At the beach entrance, you'll find a cluster of beach shacks and restaurants as well as a volleyball court. Most of the restaurants and bars line the road near the beach, with the area around the Centro Comercial being the closest thing to a social focal point. If you're looking to get in the

Whale watching

Humpback whales have used the Dominican Republic's Samaná Bay and Silver Bank coral reef sanctuary as a nursery and breeding ground for untold millennia. Taino drawings on the limestone caves of Los Haitises depict breaching whales in the Bahía de Samaná, and Columbus made note of their presence here in 1493. The whales return each December after spending nine months fanning out across the North Atlantic in search of enormous quantities of food; by late January, more than twelve thousand of them, the entire northern Atlantic population, move around the waters of the country's Northeast Coast. They're at their liveliest in Samaná's tepid depths, as males track females, compete for attention and engage in courting displays, while mothers teach their calves basic survival skills. Don't allow yourself to come here during the winter without taking an expedition to see them; the season generally runs from mid-January to mid-March. Whale Samaná/Victoria Marine, Malecón (☎ & ℱ 538-2494; US$45, advance reservations required), offers excellent whale tours.

water and do a bit more than swim, Dive Samaná (℡538-0210; RD\$1500/dive), who operate out of a beach shack by the *Casa Marina Bay* but are totally independent, organize **diving** trips around the tip of the peninsula to reefs, wrecks and even caves, including an underwater cave with an air pocket known as La Catedral. By the beach, Rancho Thikis, in front of the *Casa Marina Bay*, offers **horseriding** trips along the shore for US\$10/hr as well as whole- and half-day trips.

Playa Rincón

30km northeast of Samaná. Hidden from the rest of the peninsula, Playa Rincón is one of the top Samaná beaches; a pity then that it's so inaccessible, with only one rocky road leading to it from Las Galeras and several ferry rides that make the trip, either daily or by charter, including one that departs at 9am from Dive Samaná on Calle Las Galeras (US\$10). Tucked away at the base of the Bahía de Rincón – which is buttressed on both sides by enormous capes – the beach has long been a favourite of wealthy Dominican city-dwellers who camp out here with their families.

Of all the warm, clear waters on the island, Rincón has the very finest – moderately deep

with manageable waves and a bright turquoise transparency that can't be matched – combined with a four-kilometre stretch of whiter-than-white sand and a sprawling coconut forest behind it. The entrance to the beach is near its western end, which is bordered by high cliffs. From here it's another 1km west to **Río Frío**, a freezing-cold river popular for washing off the salt at the end of the day. To the east, the beach stretches uninterrupted for another 3km – you're likely to find nary another soul as you walk its length. There are a few fresh-fish shacks set up by the Río Frío and also one to the east of the entrance, which is the most popular (around RD\$200 per head).

Las Terrenas

Midway on the peninsula's northern coast. Over the past 25 years, this former fishing village has grown from backwater to an expat-dominated resort town renowned for its buoyant nightlife. The town's Calle Principal – along with the beach – is lined with restaurants, bars and shops. The inland Dominican barrio has been built up into a warren of rough roads with dirt-cheap housing to accommodate the masses of workers needed to sustain the tourism, which hits its peak during July and August, swamped mainly by Europeans. The larger hotels and resorts catch most of the traffic but there are enough independent travellers and backpackers

▲ PLAYA RINCÓN

to keep the smaller bars and restaurants busy; and everybody tends to come together later in the evening, packing the livelier bars and discos until the early hours.

▲ LAS TERRENAS

Aside from spectacular day-trips to the surrounding countryside, the beach, which stretches uninterrupted 2km in either direction from town, is the focus of daytime entertainment. The ocean here is calm and perfect for swimming, with a coral reef 100m out that provides decent snorkelling.

Just west of the Calle Principal is a slightly less lively beach area called **Playa Las Ballenas**, named for three oblong islands in the waters just beyond it that resemble breaching humpback whales.

Playa Bonita

5km west of Las Terrenas. All Caribbean beaches promise paradise – Playa Bonita delivers. Some 13km of uninterrupted beach features the kind of powdery white sand you might expect to see only in tourist brochures, plus the offshore reef provides the best snorkelling on the peninsula. It's seen a fair bit of development over the past few years, but most of it has thankfully been discreet and tasteful, increasing the number of places to stay and eat without detracting too much from the unspoilt character. Stay the night and the sunset will leave you reeling, as will the canopy of stars. From Playa Bonita's

entrance, a sand road provides access for four-wheel-drives and motorbikes, past the front of a few hotels and behind a beachfront populated at most by one or two people taking advantage of the isolation to swim or sunbathe nude.

Playa Cosón

6km west of Playa Bonita; follow signs on dirt road to Casa Cosón. The small fishing village of Playa Cosón has two gourmet beach shacks with tables and chairs on the sand, serving grilled, fresh-caught fish for a few pesos – plus a new all-inclusive hotel complex on the outskirts. The splendid beach unfolds uninterrupted for 7km with no human outposts to speak of, before eventually running smack into the Cordillera Samaná. At the end there are a few fishing huts and a walking path leading into the mountains.

El Limón waterfall

11km east of Las Terrenas. Little more than a crossroads with a few shacks attached, dusty El Limón seems unpromising at first, but it does make an ideal base for excursions to the magnificent El Limón waterfall to the south. Upon arrival you'll be beset by several local *buscones* trying to steer you to one of the

▲ EL LIMÓN WATERFALL

excursion outfits. It is extremely important that you do not sign on for an excursion with an outfit that is not recommended in this guide. Several local outfits are really scams intended to rip off tourists. Best of the legitimate operators is Casa Santi (☎452-9352; US$25), just south of the crossroads on the road to Samaná, who include an enormous lunch in the price.

The waterfall is accessible by horse from town and takes 2.5 hours round-trip. The path cuts across a broad river before climbing into the palm-thick mountains. As the waterfall comes into sight, the horses are tethered at a small waystation and you'll need to walk the rest of the way. It's well worth the effort to see the 50m of torrential white water dropping precipitously off a sheer cliff in the middle of the wilderness. At the base of the falls is a large swimming hole.

Playa La Entrada and Playa Diamante

80km west of Samaná. The sparsely populated Playa La Entrada has a small town of the same name perched at its northern end. The sands extend from the picturesque mouth of the Río La Entrada, 10km in each direction.

Just outside town is **Lago el Dudu**, a freshwater sinkhole created by drooping volcanic rock, and used as a local swimming hole. Surrounded by dense rainforest vegetation and accessible by a series of rough steps hewn into the rock face, the place has the feel of a Tarzan movie set.

Northwest of La Entrada, the riptide-laden waters are safe only for strong swimmers until Playa Diamante, 10km north of La Entrada, with a placid, blue beach cove set off from the ocean by a rocky outcrop at its mouth.

Cabrera

5km north of Playa Diamante. Cabrera is the most visibly prosperous outpost along this part of the coastline – clean, uncongested and dotted with a number of attractive, pastel-coloured homes – but there's still precious little to it. Its city beach, Playa Clara, at the north end of town, isn't bad, though no competition for Playa Diamante, within easy striking distance. Better is the large **waterfall** just west of town, hidden off an unmarked dirt road across the C-5; the pool at its base is swimmable when the water level is high enough.

Accommodation

Acaya

Playa Bonita ☎240-6161, ☏240-6166. Modern hotel that sits right on a pretty beach, and offers a/c and all the amenities, including swimming pool, free snorkelling gear and a thatch-roofed beachside restaurant with good seafood. Go for the second-floor rooms, which are cooler and have better views. US$45–60.

Atlantis

Playa Bonita ☎ 240-6111, ☏ 240-6205, ✉ hotel.atlantis@verizon.net.do. The best accommodation on Playa Bonita, this isolated hotel has attractive, palatial rooms; try to book either the Jamaica or the Grenada room, both with panoramic views of the beach. The French restaurant on the grounds is run by the former chef of President Mitterand – at the very least try breakfast, as it's included in the price. US$53–70.

Bahía View

Av Circunvalación, Samaná ☎ 538-2186. Exceptionally clean budget hotel with a friendly proprietor and better-than-average rooms, private showers and, as the name suggests, a good view over the bay. Far and away the best option for budget travellers. US$15–25.

Casa Lotus

Beach Rd West, Las Galeras ☎ 538-0119. Untamed but beautiful terraced gardens and the kind of tranquil karma usually reserved for Buddhist monasteries make this the ideal place for those wanting absolute serenity. Inside, the Lotus offers choice rooms with hot-water baths in a beautiful beach home adorned with New Age paraphernalia. Vegetarian meals are a speciality and available upon request. US$35–60.

Casa Marina Bay

Beach Rd East, Las Galeras ☎ 538-0020, ☏ 538-0038, ☻ www.amhsamarina.com. A large, but tasteful, all-inclusive one mile east of the main road. The 200 well-equipped, smartly decorated rooms are surrounded by nice gardens and a large pool area. The standard buffet fare isn't that inspiring but the stunning white-sand beach more than makes up for it. US$90–115.

Catalina

Calle La Catalina, Cabrera ☎ 589-7700, ☏ 589-7550, ☻ www.lacatalina .com. A large country inn perched atop a steep cliff that overlooks Cabrera and the sea. The outdoor patio dining room serves excellent, pricey French cuisine (reservations necessary). They also offer local tours, including horseback riding excursions and deep-sea fishing. US$35–60.

Las Cayenas

Calle Playa Las Ballenas, Las Terrenas ☎ 240-6080, ☏ 240-6070. A popular American hang-out, *Las Cayenas* is an authentic-looking beachfront manor that resembles a grand old plantation house, with a sleepy palm-shaded patio area. Basic but elegant rooms with ceiling fans, hot water and great sea views. It's powered by solar panels, and a hearty breakfast is included in the price. US$40–50.

Costa Las Ballenas

Playa Bonita ☎ 240-6066, ☏ 240-6107, ✉ b.lasballenas@verizon .net.do. The newest Playa Bonita accommodation, this special place offers beautifully decorated individual cabañas set in a brilliant garden. Highlights include open-air showers and carefully thought-out lighting in each room. US$70–85.

Gran Bahía

Samaná–Las Galeras Rd, Samaná ☎538-3111, ⓕ538-2764, ⓦwww.occidental-hotels.com. One of the great gems among Caribbean resorts, with a majestic oceanfront setting, immaculate grounds, well-maintained rooms, a swimming pool, watersports equipment and horse stables. Reasonably priced, too, and you can sometimes get a room even cheaper through a package deal. US$50–70.

Juan y Lolo Rent House

Beach Rd West, Las Galeras ☎ & ⓕ538-0208, ⓦwww.juanylolo.com. A selection of rustic but rather attractive thatched, creole-style self-contained houses that sleep two, four or even six people. Well equipped, with spacious lounges, full-sized bathrooms and fully functional kitchens, and wonderfully peaceful. The price depends on the size of the house that you're renting. US$35–120.

Tropic Banana

Calle Playa Las Ballenas, Las Terrenas ☎240-6110, ⓕ240-6112, ⓔhotel.tropic@verizon.net.do. The oldest hotel in Las Terrenas, and still one of the very best. The well-kept rooms are large, with private balconies, and the extensive palm-covered grounds include a swimming pool and tennis court. It's also attached to a diving centre and has a peaceful bar/restaurant area. US$70–100.

Tropical Lodge

Samaná Malecón, just east of downtown ☎538-2480, ⓕ538-2068, ⓦwww.tropical-lodge.com. Easily one of the best hotels on the peninsula, this place exudes a faded colonial charm but still has modern rooms, hot showers, cable TV, a very nice swimming pool, bay views and attentive service. Set right on the water near the centre of town, just far enough away from the noise. US$50–80.

Villa Serena

Beach Rd West, Las Galeras ☎538-0000, ⓕ538-0009, ⓦwww.villaserena.com. Housed in a beautiful faux-Victorian mansion with a large, manicured tropical garden, this place just screams "honeymoon". Set right on the beach and facing a small desert island, it's difficult to imagine a more idyllic location. Try to reserve the room with the wraparound verandah facing the ocean. The restaurant (see p.94) is one of the best in town. US$105–150.

Villas Eva Luna

Calle Playa Las Ballenas, Las Terrenas ☎978-5611, ⓕ240-5704, ⓦwww.villa-evaluna.com. Five well-appointed villas that sleep up to four, with private terraces, full kitchens and king-sized beds, on quiet grounds set 200 metres off the western beach. The two larger villas have a/c. The best part here is the food, prepared by a gourmet French chef in the *table d'hôte* tradition: guests tell the chef what they want 24 hours in advance and it's prepared for the evening meal. Price depends on the size of the villa, and whether or not it has a/c. US$30–180.

Restaurants

Café de Paris

Samaná. French-run hang-out serving up delicious pizzas and crepes from around RD$80, amid colourful, Pop Art decor. At night you can check out the *boule* games played by local expats.

Cayuco

Las Terrenas. Probably the best of the clatch of excellent restaurants set in the old fisherman's village, with a bevy of excellent seafood dishes including grilled shrimp in lime sauce and seared dorado with passion fruit and plantains, for about US$35 per person. Also a pretty hopping nightspot.

Chez Nadine

Calle Principal in a tiny plaza just north of Scotiabank, Las Terrenas. This new French bakery and *salon de thé*, run by a former Parisian master baker, is a godsend. The pastries and croissants are simply unbelievable; try the lemon tart, chocolate mousse with passion fruit, or the caramel and walnut pastries, then lie down for a few hours to digest. Also a good spot for coffee or tea.

Comedor Jahaira

Las Terrenas. The place for *comida criolla* in Las Terrenas, and incredibly inexpensive. Best are Dominican standards like rice with beans and chicken, but the *mofongo* and *pescado con coco* are excellent as well. From the town centre, head up the Carretera Las Terrenas and take the second dirt track on the right after the Centro Comercial. There are three small comedores on the block – *Jahaira* is the one in the pink building.

Coyobar

Las Terrenas. Out-of-this-world pastas, especially the spaghetti vongole (clam sauce), served in this bar attached to the *Coyomar*

hotel. A terrific spot for authentic Italian cooking and great wine.

Don Juan

Tropical Lodge Hotel, Malecón just east of downtown, Samaná. A mix of French and local cuisine, including grilled lobster, giant shrimp in a delicious lime sauce, beef tenderloin in pepper gravy, grilled fish in a passion-fruit sauce and young goat curry, all at a reasonable US$20 per person. They also have a top-notch wine cellar, though a bottle will double the price of your meal.

Kanesh Village

Calle Playa Las Ballenas, 200m back from the beach, just west of Las Terrenas ⊕240-6333. It's worth going out of your way for some of the excellent and authentic-tasting Indian food served here, including a variety of breads, chutneys, tandoori grills and curries. Dinner needs to be reserved and ordered at least one day in advance.

Le France

Malecón, Samaná. Reasonably priced gourmet Dominican dishes with some French fare as well, in a relaxed open-air patio. The gambas (either creole or

▲ CAFÉ DE PARIS

garlic) are wonderful and the chocolate cake's to die for. Also the best people-watching spot on the waterfront.

Pescador

Las Galeras. Only open in winter. The best fish in town served on a friendly outdoor patio, 500m from the beach. The friendly Spanish proprietor is well known for his excellent hospitality and will probably join you for a customary tipple of local firewater.

Ruby

Las Galeras. Dominican seafood restaurant just off the beach with basic but very good fish, lobster, *lambí* and shrimp in creole and garlic sauces, or just roasted with lemon. Provides a nicer space to sit down and enjoy your meal than is available at the Dominican kitchen shacks along the beach, and the prices are still quite reasonable at US$10 per person. The *chillo* (red snapper) is wonderful.

Villa Serena

Las Galeras. Delicious, creative French restaurant within the best hotel in Las Galeras, with a serenely beautiful view of the hotel gardens and the sea. Culinary highlights include shrimp in papaya sauce, caramelized lobster, and lamb marinated in honey for around US$40 per person – and definitely worth it. Visitors can dine here provided it's not fully booked by hotel guests.

Virginia

El Bretón, just east of Cabrera. Outstanding little seafood restaurant just off the highway, on the patio of a private local home. They feature traditional creole, garlic or fried

preparations of super-fresh red snapper, dorado or shrimp. All plates come with heaping portions of platanos, red beans and rice. Very inexpensive at around US$8 per person.

Wasabi

Las Terrenas. New Japanese restaurant with very fresh sushi and sashimi using local fish, plus teriyaki dishes for those averse to raw seafood; wash it down with a choice from a wide selection of sakes. Look to spend around US$30 per person. Nice beachfront location, too, which is especially pleasant at night.

Bars

Bar

Playa Cosón. This idyllic thatch-roofed bar-without-a-name sits squat in the middle of paradise, with a hammock from which you can stare out all day and night onto some of the most beautiful beach and mountain scenery anywhere in the world, with nary an all-inclusive in sight. Good selection of beer and tropical drinks.

Gri Gri

Las Galeras. Right in the heart of what action exists in Las Galeras by night, this great little French-owned bar sits 200 metres off the beach and offers ice-cold beer, a decent set of house wines and some great grilled meat and fish dishes for around RD$150. This is a major gathering spot for French expats, particularly when an important soccer game is on.

Indiana Café

Las Terrenas. Beachfront bar that's always crowded but maintains a pleasantly relaxed atmosphere.

Rock music, margaritas and a great view of the water.

El Mosquito

Las Terrenas. A small but amiable outdoor bar that plays mostly Dominican music but is generally crowded with expats and foreign tourists. Best of all, you can dip your feet in the sea while you drink.

Paco Pasha

At the eastern end of an old row of fishing shacks, Las Terrenas. Popular bar-grill with tables right on the sand and a beach-volleyball net. This place is much larger than the other beachfront bars and draws very big crowds in high season – come here first if you want high-octane hedonism.

Plaza Mimi

Samaná. A set of seafront liquor and food shacks on the main rotunda that make for an extremely relaxing way to pass an evening. Expect a cacophony of competing merengue boom boxes, plenty of Cuba libres, some friendly locals and maybe even some impromptu live guitar music.

Syroz Bar

Las Terrenas. Small beach bar that's a major local hang-out. The music, a mix of really good Brazilian music and Arabesque (electronica with Middle Eastern influences), makes this the most chilled place to hang out along the beach at night. Relaxed atmosphere, great crowd and even better tropical drinks.

Clubs and entertainment

Cachet

Av Rosario Sánchez at the main traffic circle, Samaná. Cover RD$30. A fun, massive rough-and-tumble Dominican dancefloor that's been popular here for over a decade and still pulls in the biggest crowds. This is the best spot on the peninsula to see what authentic Dominican nightlife is all about. A food stand outside sells RD$20 pulled-pork sandwiches.

Naomi

Samaná. Cover RD$40. Slick, dark, bustling meat market just off the waterfront with great light shows and sound system, playing a mix of merengue and American Top 40. Draws a good mix of locals, expats and tourists, and is less intimidating than the other local discos.

Nuevo Mundo

Las Terrenas, a few metres south of the town's main crossroads. Very popular club with a modern look, spinning a jarring mix of merengue and European techno. A bit seedy but still a great place to dance.

▲ NUEVO MUNDO

The Northeast Coast

The increasingly touristed Northeast Coast centres on bustling Cabarete, an oceanfront town with a host of water and adventure sports, including kiteboarding, windsurfing and mountain biking. It also boasts the best accommodations, restaurants and nightlife on the entire northern coast – though the focus on surfing has turned it into something of a haven for young, sculpted surf bums debating the nuances of gear between death-defying feats. Cabarete's older, homelier sister is Sosúa, which lies several kilometres west – once the area's major tourist town but today something akin to a faded film star slowly decaying on Sunset Boulevard. The downscale ethos has prompted a string of genuinely fun outdoor beach bars to open along Playa Sosúa, well worth a visit if you're in the area. If you seek anything approximating authentic Dominican life, however, you're best off heading well east to the pretty fishing village of Río San Juan, with a series of stunningly beautiful, under-utilized beaches, and a lagoon that offers boat tours through a mangrove swamp and a large cave. Wherever you go, you'll find plenty of hidden pleasures in the Cordillera Septentrional mountains that border the coast, including a secluded gourmet Indian restaurant, horse ranches with rides into mountain wilderness and cascade trips down a steep waterfall.

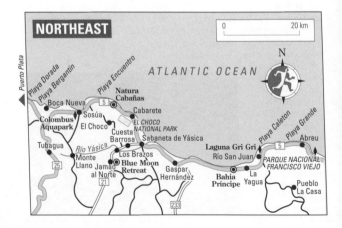

ACCOMMODATION		EATING & DRINKING					
Pensión		The Lost		On the Waterfront	1	Rocky's	6
Anneliese	C	Gringo	8	La Puntilla de		Voodoo Lounge	7
Piergiorgio Palace	A	Michael's	4	Piergiorgio	2		
Waterfront	B	Moru Mai	3	Restaurant Central	5		

Sosúa

Set along a sheltering horseshoe inlet impressed into the eastern end of Bahía de Sosúa, this large resort town was created in the late nineteenth century by the United Fruit Company. In the late 1930s, dictator Rafael Trujillo provided refuge for several hundred Jews fleeing Nazi Germany, who set up residence here. The refugees created the barrio known as **El Batey**, which is now the town's tourism hub.

Most of the action focuses on and around the junction of Calle Pedro Clisante and Calle Duarte. The Jewish legacy still remains, and one block east of Duarte, on Martínez and

Dr Rosén, you'll find the old **synagogue**, a simple wooden structure adorned with a 50-year-old Star of David, and still used by a number of practising Jewish-Dominican descendants of the settlers. There's a small museum attached, **El Museo de Sosúa** (Mon–Thurs & Sun 6–11pm; free), which recounts the early experiences of the refugees and the development of the agricultural co-operative through photographs and a few of the settlers' personal effects. Directly west of El Batey, crescent-shaped **Playa Sosúa** stretches out along the bay. Dividing the town in half, the small bay is completely placid and transparent, a contrast to

Getting there and getting around

Almost everyone arrives here via the Puerto Plata airport (see p.108), which is actually slightly closer to Sosúa than it is to Puerto Plata. The Carretera 5 that lines this part of the northern coast makes getting around by car or public transport easy. The country's two major bus companies, Caribe Tours and Metro, both ply the highway from end to end, along with guaguas and plentiful *público* taxis. All you really have to do if you want to go from town to town is stand on the highway and hold out your arm until a guagua stops. Keep in mind, though, that due to the high-volume tourism in this area, guagua rip-offs have become a real problem. For this reason, you have to agree on a price and pay *before* you get into the guagua.

▲ SOSÚA SYNAGOGUE

the crowded beach and, just behind the sand, the busy row of bars, lobster-tank restaurants and souvenir shops, with some colourful, itinerant vendors lurking among them.

To the west of the beach is **Los Charamicos**, a traditional Dominican neighbourhood with two entrances from the C-5 at its eastern and western ends – both crowded with motoconchos. At the east entrance you'll also find the informal bus stations for Caribe Tours and Transporte del Cibao.

Columbus Aquapark

2km west of Sosúa, Carretera 5 ☎571-2642. Daily 10am–6pm. RD$250 for a full day, RD$90 after 1pm. This impressive water park offers 25 different rides, including a number of slides and a thrill ride that hurls you along fake whitewater rapids through pitch darkness. There are also two dramatic high drops and a slower, winding raft ride that traverses the length of the park. It's best to go on weekdays, when the place is less crowded.

Tubagua and Tropical Plantation

20km south of Sosúa on the Carretera Turística ☎656-1210, ☎412-0585, ⊛www.plantationtropical.com. Daily 9am–5pm. US$40, US$10 extra for transport from your hotel. Tiny Tubagua is the one place worth stopping off between Sosúa and Santiago, if you happen to be headed inland. Besides a local cave system, the highlight is the new Tropical Plantation, a tourist-oriented rural ranch and flower farm that's perfect if you've got kids in tow. The tour of the grounds includes a long walk through vast fields of anthuriums, bromeliads, birds of paradise and heliconias, plus a stop in a lovely lakeside orchid sanctuary. Then it's on to the agricultural section of the plantation, which shows how traditional local crops are grown, including pineapple, banana, papaya, passion fruit and aloe vera. There's a shrub labyrinth in which you can easily get lost, a petting zoo with local farm animals, an aviary full of parrots, macaws and cockatoos, and another with butterflies. The best part, though, is the peace and quiet amid stunning natural surroundings. All in all, a great way to spend a half day.

Cabarete

10km east of Sosúa. Stretched between the beach and lagoon that bear its name, the crowded international enclave

▲ COLUMBUS AQUAPARK

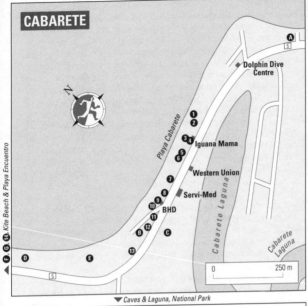

ACCOMMODATION		EATING & DRINKING			
Agualina	G	Le Bistro	10	Friends	11
Azzurro Club	E	Las Brisas	3	José O'Shay's	7
Cabarete Beach		Casa del		Lax	9
Houses	D	Pescador	8	Onno's	5
Cita del Sol	C	La Casita	6	Panadería	
El Magnifico	A	DND	4	Repostería Dick	12
Natura Cabañas	F	eXtreme Bar	14	Pitú	2
Villa Taina	B	Eze	1	Village Jazz Club	13

of Cabarete owes its existence almost entirely to windsurfing and kiteboarding. There was no town to speak of in 1984 when legendary windsurfer Jean Laporte discovered its near-perfect watersport conditions. The town quickly became a haven for surf bums, augmented exponentially when kiteboarding joined the mix. The multicultural cross-section of aficionados of the sport draws a growing community of people from across the globe, which has in turn attracted hotel chains and an assortment of adventure-sports outfits. A spate of all-inclusives has led to more traditional tourism, but the clients at these new hotels are generally younger, hipper and more interested in adventure sports than guests at more family-oriented complexes like *Playa Dorada*.

As you'd expect from a town that grew up on surfing, the beach, **Playa Cabarete**, is where the real action is. During the day it's crowded with windsurfers, kiteboarders and sun-worshippers, although if you head out a little way east or west you'll find it a bit more peaceful, except at **Kite Beach**,

Windsurfing and kiteboarding in Cabarete

The conditions for windsurfing in Cabarete are so perfect that the whole bay may as well have been designed specifically with this in mind. The trade winds normally blow from the east, meaning that they sweep across the bay from right to left allowing easy passage both out to the offshore reefs and back to the beach. Downwind, the waters lap onto the amusingly named **Bozo Beach**, which will catch anybody unfortunate to have a mishap. The offshore reef provides plenty of surf for the experts who ride the waves, performing tricks and some incredibly spectacular jumps. The reef also shelters the inshore waters so that on all but the roughest of winter days the waters remain calm. During the morning the winds are little more than a gentle breeze and this, coupled with the flat water, makes the bay ideal for beginners, especially in summer when the surface can resemble a mirror. Then, as the temperature rises, the trade winds kick in big-time and the real show begins. Take some binoculars if you want to see the action out on the reef.

The white-sand Kite Beach has become a massive international hub for the relatively new sport of **kiteboarding**. In many ways similar to windsurfing, but relying on a huge kite to provide the power instead of a sail, kiteboarding needs less wind to really get moving and the best riders, as they're called, perform huge jumps and tricks that would be impossible with a sail. In the third week of June, Kite Beach plays host to the prestigious Kiteboarding World Cup. Good old-fashioned surfing has also become increasingly popular, especially along Playa Encuentro west of town (see below).

All the windsurf outfitters (see p.172) are based right along the beach, in the heart of the activity. They have a confusing array of pricing structures but there's not really much between them all when you break it down. The main differences are the actual make (rather than quality) of equipment, the amount of gear in stock (important mainly during busier times like Christmas–New Year and July–August), the launch position on the beach, and the languages spoken by the staff. Most also run kiteboard schools here too, although there are others specializing in the latter on Kite Beach itself. If you need any equipment repaired while you're here, ask for Pablito at Fanatic (see p.172); he does great work for a reasonable price.

2km west of the town centre, where hundreds of kiteboarders rule the shoreline. At night, the bars and restaurants spill onto the sand, making for a superb dining scene, where you can eat at a quality restaurant with sand between your toes and the sound of the sea as background music. It also gets pretty lively later as the music gets louder and many of the bars take on the role of discos and clubs.

Behind the town, the lush, green **El Choco National Park** contains the lovely Laguna Cabarete, home to thousands of birds, but surrounded by dense brush and somewhat hard to get around. The park also holds the Caves of Cabarete, a set of holes around the lagoon that have been fenced off and illuminated with electric light. There's a park entrance down a well-marked turnoff just west of town, where you can join an organized tour (Mon–Fri 9am–5pm; RD$350) to the caves and lagoon; Iguana Mama (see p.167) runs tours as well. You'll see a few "Arawak glyphs", though twentieth-century graffiti is more prominent than Taino art, and also get the opportunity to swim in an underground pool. Self-guided exploration of the national park isn't really an option as there's not much trail-marking and the odds of ending up lost and confused are relatively high.

▲ BLUE MOON RETREAT

Playa Encuentro

4km west of Cabarete on the C-5, then north on an unmarked turnoff at a metal gate. Undeveloped Playa Encuentro features massive waves unseen in most of the DR, which attract a good number of surfers and a handful of highly skilled, clearly suicidal kiteboarders. It's worth stopping off between 6am and 8am to watch the most daring of them ride atop six-metre waves, execute 360-degree leaps and even ride within the curl of the waves when the surf is large enough to allow it.

El Choco bike trail

The main attraction in Cabarete's surrounding countryside is the mountain-biking trail along the old El Choco Road, which was once used to truck bananas from the countryside to the coast but is now little more than a dirt path. Iguana Mama's (see p.167) US$40 half-day mountain-bike excursion down El Choco is a fairly challenging trip that steers you through the heart of rural DR. The trail starts approximately 4km west of Cabarete at the dirt road just before the Colmado Beatón. This rough track is known as La Bombita, and it feeds into the larger El Choco, from which it's

17km past nonstop breathtaking mountain scenery dotted with tiny Dominican outposts to the pueblo La Catalina. From there the trip heads down the gorgeous Moca Road to Sabaneta de Yásica, then back along the coast to Cabarete. Some half-day trips take you back by boat along a remote stretch of the Río Islabón.

Sabaneta de Yásica and around

8km southeast of Cabarete. Sabaneta de Yásica is a nondescript concrete town at the junction of the Río Yásica – a large river with little development along it – and the Atlantic. Jungle River Tours, a few metres west of town (☎249-5906; US$35), operates a **rainforest ecotour** that takes small groups up a Yásica tributary to the large Laguna Islabón, then turns back along the Yásica to the river's mouth. This two and a half hour ride cruises through otherwise impossible-to-access, dense rainforest and mangrove swamp, home to an enormous variety of orchids, tropical birds and reptiles.

South from Sabaneta de Yásica, the **Sabaneta–Moca Road** winds through the heart of the Cordillera Septentrional mountains past a number of relatively prosperous agricultural pueblos. At pueblo Los Brazos, the *Blue Moon Retreat* (☎223-0614, ⓦ www .bluemoonretreat.net; US$35), is an isolated mountaintop compound, with a few brightly decorated cabins, featuring the work of local artists, scattered around a swimming pool. Even more notable is their unique restaurant, which serves delicious multi-course gourmet Indian dinners in an expansive tent on mats and cushions. Reservations, which are for the whole evening, have to be made at least three days in advance, and they only serve parties of ten or more people; if short of the requisite number, see if you can piggyback onto another party (try at Iguana Mama or any of the windsurfing schools). The whole trip including return transport from Cabarete is usually around US$50.

Río San Juan and Laguna Gri-Gri

40km east of Sabaneta de Yásica. The small, friendly fishing village of Río San Juan borders the large mangrove lagoon, Laguna Gri-Gri, as well as several relatively undeveloped beaches – though with a slew of high-end resorts in the works. You'd be forgiven for wanting the town's tree-lined streets, easy-going atmosphere and simple reliance on boat building, fishing and dairy farming to remain forever as they are. The centre of transportation and activity is the Texaco station on the corner of the C-5 and Calle Duarte, behind which is an outdoor bar well placed for people watching.

North up Duarte, the main thoroughfare lined with shops,

hotels, taxi stands and a post office, you'll hit the part of town most come to see: Laguna Gri-Gri, a magnificent mangrove preserve traversed by organized boat tours boarded from a small quay at the road's end. The ninety-minute tours, which cost RD$900 per boatload (up to 15 people), begin at the pond on the northern end of Duarte; go early in the morning for better birdwatching. Beyond the lagoon, the boats enter a series of impressive coastal caves, then head along the coast to Playa Caletón for a quick swim. You can arrange for snorkelling (for another RD$500) if you ask before the boat sets off. You can also see the lagoon's birdlife by walking east from the *Bahía Blanca Hotel* to the peninsular bird sanctuary that the tour skirts. It's also worth heading west to the barrio of Acapulco, a residential neighbourhood of unpaved roads and front lawns adorned with carved wooden boats, which artisans here craft for local fishermen. A five-minute walk west of town is the *Bahía Príncipe* resort's private beach, which can be sneaked onto from either side of its fenced-off grounds, although better beaches lie east of town.

Playa Caletón and Playa Grande

1km east of Río San Juan; accessible from the C-5 by a marked turnoff. A small cove surrounded by rocks, Playa Caletón is a lovely little beach that's safe for swimming and much frequented by locals. Two kilometres further east, though, is Playa Grande, by far the most spectacular in the area, a long strip of spotless white sand flanked by high cliffs and crashing surf. As a result of the strong surf and frequent undertows, it's more majestic than it is swimmer friendly, and you're best off staying on the sand, where you'll find vendor stalls at the eastern end selling sandwiches, snacks and pineapple-filled rum drinks.

Cabo Francisco Viejo and Playa El Bretón

10km east of Playa Grande. Park: Mon–Fri 10am–4.30pm. RD$40. The small national park of Cabo Francisco Viejo spreads out between the sister towns of Abreu and El Bretón. It centres on a majestic cape with a lighthouse and is a great place to take a short stroll and look out over the ocean. Just east of the cape and protected from development is the pounding surf of Playa El Bretón, a ruggedly beautiful beach backed by high, chalk-white cliffs.

Accommodation

Agualina

West of the main strip, Carretera 5, Cabarete ☎571-0805, ⊛www .agualina.com. Lovely full-service apartments right on Kite Beach, and with an in-house (Dare2Fly) kiteboarding school. Unlike most similar places, these are not only spacious and

comfortable, they're also stylishly done. Highly recommended if you're going to spend most of your time on Kite Beach. US$85–125.

Pensión Anneliese

Calle Dr Rosén at the ocean, Sosúa ☎ & ☞571-2208, ⊛www.weblatino. de/pension. A quiet hotel with pretty, fenced-in grounds and a view of the water. The large rooms have oceanfront balconies, and there's a secluded pool in back. Breakfast is available for RD$100. US$15–50.

Azzurro Club

West of the main strip, Carretera 5, Cabarete ☎571-4000, ☞571-4545, ⊛www.starzresorts.com. One of the first all-inclusives to open up in Cabarete; its designers went to great pains to integrate with the town, abandoning the usual high walls in favour of an open courtyard entrance. The food's pretty basic but you're close enough to a plethora of other eating options. Rooms are large and have a/c and TV. US$100–140.

Bahía Blanca

Calle Deligne at Playa Río San Juan, Río San Juan ☎589-2562, ☞589-2528. Set on a sandy beach, this small independent hotel in the heart of town offers a spectacular sunrise/sunset view off the water from its terrace dining room. Clean, comfortable rooms come with fridge and ceiling fan, and there's one basement room for only RD$350, the best bargain in the area. US$30–35.

Bahía Príncipe

Carretera 5, 6km west of Río San Juan ☎226-1590, ☞226-1991, ⊛www .bahia-principe.com. Behemoth

▲ BAHÍA BLANCA

all-inclusive that manages to remain pretty and secluded, marked by a long row of pastel bars at its entrance that stay open until 4am nightly. Inside the inner gates are several hundred villas, a private beach, casino, spa, supermarket, car rental and exceptional children's facilities. US$65–85.

Cabarete Beach Houses

1km west of the main strip, Carretera 5, Cabarete ☏ 571-0744, ☏ 571-0655, ⓦ www.cabaretebeachhouses .com. Excellent high-end value, especially if you're with a group: these two-storey apartments boast two huge bedrooms, a spacious lounge, well-equipped kitchens and top floors with private roof terraces. Located on a quiet section of beach with a private pool and a tennis court. US$100–140.

Cita del Sol

Carretera 5, downtown Cabarete ☏ 571-0720, ☏ 571-0795, ⓦ www .citadelsol.com. A special spot, far enough away from the road to cut out most of the chaos yet right on the beach and next to several restaurants. Good-sized rooms with kitchens and a pleasant pool area. They also rent full-service apartments with modern, well-appointed kitchens and bathrooms. US$50–85.

El Magnífico

East of the main strip, Carretera 5, Cabarete ☏ & ☏ 571-0868, ⓦ www .hotelmagnifico.com. Three different beachside buildings with eye-catching architecture and ethnic interiors set around a soothing pool area. The rooms are truly outstanding – plenty of elbow room and everything looks brand new. Tranquil, yet it's just a five-minute stroll

from the town centre. Perfect for relaxing in the morning and surfing in the afternoon. US$60–85; larger rooms with kitchen US$85–150.

Natura Cabañas

5km west of Cabarete within the Perla Marina gated community ☏ 571-1507, ⓦ www.naturacabana.com. On a private beach, super-nice, super-secluded set of bungalows with kitchenettes and strong hot water, aiming for a primitive ambience but with modern amenities like hair dryers. Many come here for the extensive spa facilities, which include steam bath with aromatherapy, mud baths, seaweed wraps, facials, steam room and massage. On top of that, they also have a very highly regarded Chilean seafood restaurant on the grounds. A great place to get away from it all. US$60–110, depending on the size of the cabaña.

Piergiorgio Palace Hotel

La Puntilla 2, Sosúa ☏ 571-2626, ☏ 571-2786, ⓦ www.piergiorgiohotel .com. All-inclusive resort in a faux-Victorian manor. Big, high-ceilinged, high-standard rooms with all the amenities, and two meals daily at the excellent La Puntilla restaurant. Best location in El Batey. US$90–135.

Villa Taina

Carretera 5, downtown Cabarete ☏ 571-0722, ☏ 571-0883, ⓦ www .villataina.com. One of the best hotels in town with a smart reception area, helpful staff and a selection of very clean, tidy and imaginatively decorated rooms, with a/c, phones, luxurious bathrooms and good beds. Rooms with balconies and sea views are pricier. US$70–125.

Waterfront
Dr Rosén 1, Sosúa ☎571-2760, ☎571-3586. Modern bungalows with private hot-water bath in a stunning position just off the sea. The sweeping ocean terrace with swimming pool is a big plus. US$25–45.

Restaurants

▲ WATERFRONT RESTAURANT

Casa del Pescador
Carretera 5, downtown Cabarete. The best seafood in town in an idyllic candlelit atmosphere right on the beach. All meals come with sides of ratatouille, rice, french fries and a small salad. Watch out for the extremely strong free rum aperitif.

La Casita
Carretera 5, downtown Cabarete. Festive main-strip restaurant notable for its gargantuan skillets of grilled langostinas, which are not to be missed. Hold out for a beachfront table, as the setting is especially pleasant. Prices are relatively high at around US$35–40 per person, but it's worth it.

El Corral
The lagoon entrance, Río San Juan. Best restaurant in town, with a small patio and Spanish specialities, including a great paella chock-full of all manner of ocean life and spicy *chorizo*, *calamari romana* and a fish of the day special with beer and dessert for only RD$225.

Eze
Carretera 5, downtown Cabarete. Mellow beachfront eatery offering California wraps (try the shrimp, avocado and yoghurt

sauce), smoothies and fresh fruit juice. Great lunch idea if you've been on the water all morning. During the early evening hours this is also a good spot to come for a frozen tropical drink.

Friends
Carretera 5, downtown Cabarete. Next door to *Panadería Dick*, this very popular breakfast and lunch spot serves up hearty sandwiches, salads and fruit shakes. Great banana pancakes, plus fresh muffins and cookies for those on the go.

Le Bistro
On a small unnamed lane within a strip mall in the town center, Cabarete. Authentic country French cooking at reasonable prices, with an emphasis on the fresh local seafood. Specialities include duck breast with honey sauce, *calamari provençal*, fish fondue with four sauces, and chocolate mousse.

Moru Mai
Calle Pedro Clisante, El Batey, Sosúa. Decent, affordable international fare in a smartly decorated diner. The chic and convivial atmosphere makes it popular with the twenty-something crowd, and the service is excellent.

On the Waterfront
Dr Rosén 1, El Batey, Sosúa. Terrific

PLACES The Northeast Coast

seafood restaurant on a sweeping oceanfront patio; choose from fresh lobster, red snapper, sea bass, *lambí* and *calamari*. Not as swank as *La Puntilla* (see below) but just as good and a notch less expensive.

Panadería Repostería Dick

Carretera 5, downtown Cabarete. Closed evenings and Wed afternoon. Just the smell of this place will give you a new lease on life, with various gourmet breads for a few pesos, great Danishes and croissants as good as those in Paris. They also have fresh-squeezed orange juice and their cappuccinos taste like French *café crème*.

Pitú

Carretera 5, downtown Cabarete. A favourite with the international workforce, this casual eatery on the beach features a good selection of pizza and Mexican dishes from RD$90, along with great coffee. The chicken stir-fry is especially good.

La Puntilla de Piergiorgio

La Puntilla 1, El Batey, Sosúa. Sosúa's best-known restaurant (though standards have slipped in the past few years) set along a series of seven grand waterfront patios that showcase jaw-dropping sunsets. The seafood is particularly good, including the lobster. It's the dearest option in town, though a free aperitif is included in the meal.

Restaurant Central

Calle Kunhardt and Arzeno, Los Charamicos, Sosúa. A phenomenally popular little Dominican fish restaurant. It's well worth the wait (up to a half-hour), though, for the specialities with *criolla* sauce. Served with the traditional Dominican accompaniments, but a good bit less greasy than usual.

Bars

DND (Do Not Disturb)

Carretera 5, downtown Cabarete. The latest hot spot, this tapas bar has a super-comfortable lounge with couches and ambient electronica. The effect really works – a hedonistic party atmosphere that manages to actually be relaxing. The food is excellent too, including reasonably priced Thai food like coconut curry shrimp and pad thai.

José O'Shay's

Carretera 5, downtown Cabarete. Chain Irish bar that's inexplicably popular with the North American crowd, who come here to get tanked and sing along with American barroom "classics" like *Free Bird*, just like they do back home! Drinks are overpriced but there are always a lot of people crammed inside – and there's the obligatory Guinness on tap to go with sangría and other tropical cocktails.

Lax

Carretera 5 at the western end of downtown Cabarete. An inviting spot to start out the evening, *Lax* is loaded with a row of couches that look out onto the sea and is a relaxing place to party even when it's packed to the gills.

The Lost Gringo

Playa Sosúa at El Batey entrance, Sosúa. The most popular spot on the strip, in large part because of its enviable location near El Batey. Good frozen tropical drinks, several brands of beer and American rock.

Onno's

Carretera 5, downtown Cabarete. Lively bar/restaurant, on the beachfront in the centre of the strip, which really gets going in the small hours – plays mainly European and American hits, often offered up by relatively well-known guest DJs. They also have pretty good food, including pizzas, seared tuna filet and seafood *linguine*.

Rocky's

Dr Rosén 22, Sosúa. Friendly, crowded local watering hole with great burgers, generous slabs of barbecued ribs, ice-cold beer and their very tasty drink speciality, amaretto sour. The place is especially popular with expats, and the proprietor is something of an expert on all things Sosúan. Also has the only WIFI hot spot in Sosúa (free access to customers).

Clubs and entertainment

Bahía Príncipe Bars

Bahía Príncipe resort, 3km west of Río San Juan. One of the better nightlife scenes available at an all-inclusive, this is a long row of pastel bars and liquor shacks at the entrance to the town's big resort complex, with dancing all across the strip as well as tables where you can sit and relax as you pound down Cuba libres. A genuinely fun atmosphere, bustling until 3 or 4am nightly.

Las Brisas

Carretera 5 at the eastern end of downtown Cabarete. Traditional merengue bar on the Cabarete strip that's been here since the beginning. Not one of the town's hot spots any longer, but still a good local dance spot.

Dollaras

10km west of Cabarete and 5km south of the Carretera 5 in pueblo Monte Llano. This friendly *típico* Dominican disco, in the rural village of Monte Llano, is frequented by field hands and factory workers after a hard day's labour. A perfect place to see how people in the pueblos kick back.

eXtreme Bar

eXtreme Hotel, Kite Beach, Cabarete. Buzzing Kite Beach party zone set in a half-glassed-in bamboo bar that's perpetually crowded with visiting kiteboarders. The pool table, dancefloor, weekly movie showings and bonfire beach parties always keep things interesting, and they've generally made Kite Beach a far more fun place to stay.

Village Jazz Club

Carretera 5 just east of Villa Taina, Cabarete. Closed Mon. A top-notch little jazz club with excellent Latin-fused live music, Brazilian bossa nova and blues. The proprietor is the piano player and the clientele tends to be a little older than at the rest of the Cabarete bars. Really the only place in the DR where you can hear this kind of music at a high-quality level.

Voodoo Lounge

Martínez 1, Sosúa. Open-air late-night techno/karaoke lounge (depending on the night) set in a two-storey, octagonal building in the centre of town. Typically packed until 3am with drunken package tourists from across the globe, and the only disco in Sosúa that's not geared primarily toward prostitution.

Puerto Plata and Playa Dorada

Puerto Plata and Playa Dorada comprise the mass-tourism capital of the Caribbean, and most of the half-million-plus tourists who visit each year arrive on package tours to the walled-off vacation factory of Playa Dorada, a super-complex of self-contained all-inclusive resorts. Not to be overlooked is Puerto Plata, a kilometre east of the beach. A vibrant Dominican town of 200,000, it's well worth exploring for the historic architecture and hopping nightlife. At its core, Puerto Plata's Old City unfolds as a narrow grid of streets that was once the country's most stylish neighbourhood. Around the original town sprawls a patchwork maze of industrial zones and concrete barrios known as the New City, formed over the past century with the growth of the town's main industries outside of tourism, namely tobacco, sugar and rum.

Fort San Felipe

Overlooking the Malecón, west of Avenida Colón. 9am–noon & 2–5pm, closed Wed. RD$15. The orange-tinted limestone fort perches atop a rocky point jutting into the sea. The Spaniards constructed it in 1540 as a defence against corsairs and a prison for smugglers; when the city was torched in 1605, it was the lone structure to survive. Once past the phalanx of unnecessary freelance tour

Getting there and getting around

Aeropuerto Internacional Puerto Plata (☎ 586-0408), 18km east of Puerto Plata, is the main northern entry point into the country. While most of the more expensive hotels have shuttle buses waiting for their clients, motoconchos can also take you into town for RD$20, and there are plenty of taxis heading to points further out. Just outside the entrance to the airport is the main coastal road, Carretera 5 (C-5), stretching from Puerto Plata all the way to Samaná. From the highway you can catch a guagua going in either direction; a trip to Puerto Plata or Sosúa should cost around RD$40.

Puerto Plata is a major junction point for Caribe Tours and Metro buses, which arrive here from the south (via Santo Domingo and Santiago) and the east (via Samaná). Caribe Tours (☎ 586-4544, ✉www.caribetours.com.do) has its terminal on Avenida Pedro Clisante, between the Parque Central and the C-5. The Metro terminal, Beller and 16 de Agosto (☎586-6062), is in a residential part of town well east of the centre of activity, though still accessible by motoconcho. The guaguas that travel the length of the coast all end up at the Parque Central, from where you can pick up a taxi or motoconcho if your hotel isn't within walking distance. These can also be used to head to Playa Dorada, Costambar or Ocean World (RD$100–250).

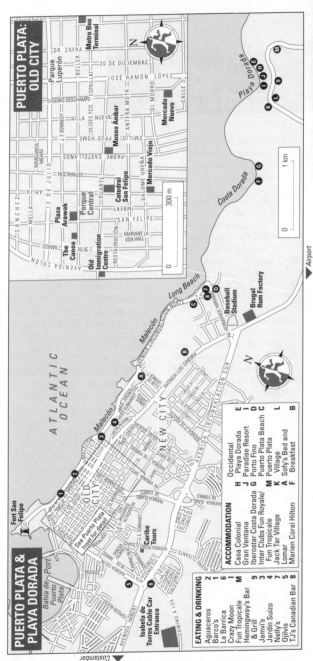

PUERTO PLATA: OLD CITY

Metro Bus Terminal
DR. ZAFRA
Parque Luperón
BELLER
20 DE DICIEMBRE
JOSÉ RAMÓN LÓPEZ
EUGENIO DESCHAMPS
VILLA NUEVA
ULISES VALDEZ
FCO. ESPAILLAT
ANTERA MOTA
EL MORRO
CALLE 2
Mercado Nuevo
J.F. KENNEDY
PRUD-HOME
EMILIO PRUD-HOME
Museo Ambar
MARGARITA MEARS
PADRE CASTELLANOS
Mercado Viejo
12 DE JULIO
SEPARACIÓN
DUARTE
SALOMÉ UREÑA
Catedral
San Felipe
SÁNCHEZ
MELLA
ARIZA
IMBERT
SAN FELIPE
Plaza Arawak
Parque Central
MARIANE LA VDA.HALL
30 DE MARZO
RESTAURACIÓN
The Canoa
Old Immigration Centre
AVENIDA COLÓN

0   300 m

0   1 km

Playa Dorada
M
E
H I O
9
L
K
Costa Dorada
F G

Airport

PLACES Puerto Plata and Playa Dorada

PUERTO PLATA & PLAYA DORADA

ATLANTIC OCEAN

Malecón

Bahía de Puerto Plata
Fort San Felipe

Long Beach

Malecón

Baseball Stadium
Brugal Rum Factory

NEW CITY
OLD CITY

See Puerto Plata Inset for detail

AVENIDA CIRCUNVALACIÓN NORTE
AVENIDA LUIS GINEBRA
AVENIDA CIRCUNVALACIÓN SUR

Isabela de Torres Cable Car Entrance

Caribe Tours

Costambar

AVENIDA IMBERT

CAMINO A LOS

ACCOMMODATION
Casa Colonial   E
Gran Ventana   I
Iberostar Costa Dorada   D
Inter Clubs Fun Royale/ C
Fun Tropicale
Jack Tar Village   K
Lomar   L
Marien Coral Hilton   B
Occidental Playa Dorada H
Paradise Resort   J
Porto Fino   G
Puerto Plata Beach   M
Puerto Plata   A
Sofy's Bed and   F
Breakfast

EATING & DRINKING
Aguaceros   2
Barco's   1
Crazy Moon   6
La Barrica   M
Fun Tropicale   9
Hemingway's Bar   3
& Grill
Jamvi's   3
Jardín Suizo   4
Nelly's   7
Ollivis   5
TJ's Canadian Bar   8

▲ CATAMARANS NEAR PUERTO PLATA

guides who surround it, you can climb up several of the towers and gun turrets, or down into the old prison cells that were in use through the time of Trujillo. Some of the most esteemed figures in Dominican history have been imprisoned here, including Juan Pablo Duarte (incarcerated in 1844 after a bungled attempt to declare himself president) and the husbands of the Mirabal sisters, who were gunned down by Trujillo's secret police after visiting their spouses in prison. The old prison houses a small museum with artefacts such as prisoner's shackles, cannonballs and coins. The museum guard will provide you with an overacted recitation of the fort's history, and will expect an RD$30 donation. Regardless of whether you take advantage of this, be sure to check out the sea views. Bordering the fort to the east is the idyllic, seaside Parque Luperón, highlighted by a horseback bronze statue of the general who ruled the country for a year from Puerto Plata.

Parque Central

Separación and Beller. In the heart of Puerto Plata's Old City sits the Parque Central, a fast-paced focal point for transport and commercial activity, where taxis, guaguas, motoconchos and public buses vie for curbside space. On the sidewalks, carts sell sugar cane, peeled fruit and all manner of cheap souvenirs. Other vendors crowd the rest of the park, selling lottery tickets or spinning tales of Taino caves just outside town. Better to head for the small patches of tranquillity among the shaded benches and the central **gazebo**, a 1960s replica of one that stood here a century earlier.

South of the park across Calle Duarte looms the large **Catedral San Felipe**, which manages to successfully blend Spanish colonial and Art Deco influences. When not in use it's usually locked tight, and the unexciting interior isn't worth the effort it takes to get the caretaker to open it. The remaining three sides of the park are surrounded by some of the best Victorian architecture in the city, notably a colossal white gingerbread mansion on the northwest corner that now serves as a Pentecostal church. Its sweeping, elevated first-floor porch spans an entire city block. On the southeast corner, the pink gingerbread at **Separación 22**, former home of a wealthy German merchant, is the city cultural centre and houses occasional local artist exhibits. The old Moorish **town hall** next door, which still serves as the office of the mayor, is the most fanciful of the park's edifices, a battered, mini-Alhambra adorned with two mock minarets. Stroll down most any nearby street to see more such buildings, though many are in partial or complete disrepair.

Museo Ámbar

Duarte 61 and Castellanos

☎586-2848, ⊛www.ambermuseum. com. Mon–Sat 9am–6pm. RD$50. The popular museum comprises two floors of insects trapped in amber and various other amber-related exhibits in a renovated 1900 mansion called Villa Bentz, built by one of the town's wealthiest German tobacco families. At the entrance, a few artefacts give you a sense of how the family lived: outside of photographs, objects on display include flower-painted porcelain, monogrammed silverware and a colourful, glazed tile corner from the original floor. The second-floor museum, though, is the main draw, a collection culled from the amber mines in the Cordillera Septentrional south of Puerto Plata, consisting of Jurassic and Triassic leaves, flowers, spiders, termites, wasps, ants and other insects, along with one small several-million-year-old lizard identical to those on the island today. There's also a gift shop with polished jewellery and chunks of raw amber for sale.

Los Mercados

Mercado Nuevo: Isabela de Torres and Villanueva. Daily 8am–9pm. Mercado Viejo: Calle Ureña and Separación. Daily 8am–6.30pm. The city's old and new markets sit just several blocks away from each other.

The **Mercado Nuevo** is housed in a decaying, concrete, star-shaped structure crammed with colourful, crowded stalls. Among the mass-produced Haitian paintings, T-shirts, lewd novelty items and maracas you'll find quality rum, Cuban cigars, and some good wicker furniture, all fairly cheap if you're willing to haggle.

The **Mercado Viejo**, where prices are not negotiable, spills onto the sidewalk from a series of former private homes and is more utilitarian, containing hardware, furniture, lawn flamingos and a *botánica*, a shop dedicated to syncretist religious items, marked by pictures and icons propped along the outside wall. This is as good as any place to learn about Dominican folk religion; ask and the owner will give you the address of one of the old-fashioned *brujos* who live in the outer barrios, syncretist folk healers who are still a staple of rural Dominican life.

Avenida Colón

Avenida Colón marks the Old City's western boundary, with nothing too much of interest beyond it – just the port and the extremely poor barrio Agua Negra. Along Colón you'll find decrepit Victorian warehouses that once held enormous loads of cargo waiting to be shipped to Europe. Despite thorough decay, much of their original ornamentation is still visible, including elegant, dangling icicle awnings on a few.

▲ VICTORIAN GINGERBREAD HOUSE

▲ LONG BEACH BAR

The Malecón

The centre of Puerto Plata social life is the two-kilometre-long Malecón, a sunny, spacious boardwalk lined with hotels and all forms of commerce. During the day it's a popular spot for locals to hang out, lie on the beach and picnic. At night bars open up and numerous restaurants and outdoor shacks serve up Dominican fast food.

The Malecón begins at Long Beach, on the town's far eastern end, not the most picturesque beach by any stretch, but with a convivial mood, peopled largely by merengue-blaring teens. Behind the sand is a concrete plaza with a tower you can climb for a wide-angle view of the coast, although this is probably not the place to hang around after dark. A row of outdoor bars extends for several hundred metres down Avenida Hermanas Mirabal, quite fun at night, though increasingly the domain of prostitutes.

Brugal Rum Factory

Circunvalación Sur, east of Hermanas Mirabal. Mon–Fri 9am–noon & 2–3.30pm. Free. The Brugal Rum bottling factory, a popular stop-off for tourists, is really little more than a PR exercise for this local rum company. Better than the quick glance at the bottling

and packing operations are the free rum-based margaritas on the outdoor patio that follow the tour.

Mount Isabela

Circunvalación Sur and Av Teleférico at far western end of town past the port ☎970-0501. 8.30am–5pm, closed Wed. Adults RD$200, children RD$100. Puerto Plata's crowning attraction is the suspended **cable car ride** that goes to the top of Mount Isabela de Torres. Though the ride has been sporadically operational over the last few years, if running, it's definitely not to be missed; the views of the city on the 25-minute trip are stupendous. At the summit a statue of **Christ the Redeemer**, a slightly downsized version of the Río de Janeiro landmark with its arms spread out over the city, crowns a manicured lawn. Also on the grounds are a tropical garden, a pricey café and a souvenir shop. The mountain is now a protected national park, covered partially by rainforest and inhabited by 32 species of indigenous bird. Don't wander beyond the area marked off for visitors, as Mount Isabela is in the process of splitting in two. The brown splotch along its face, visible from the city, is a landslide created by the split, and there are a number of deep fissures at the summit.

Playa Dorada

5km east of Puerto Plata on the C-5. Effectively walled off from the outside universe, Playa Dorada feels worlds away from the bustle of Puerto Plata. Inside its confines are fourteen separate resorts, each an entity unto itself, with restaurants, discos, swimming pools, hot tubs and an array of sports facilities. Meandering between them is one of the best golf courses in the country, designed by Robert Trent Jones.

Frequented by a half-million package tourists per year, Playa Dorada is the perfect place to lie for a few days on a beautiful beach, though those seeking more than a cruise ship on sand may find its alluring promotion campaign – like the city of gold for which it was named – a mirage.

The beach is the main draw, 2km of impeccably white sand from which you're treated to terrific views of Mount Isabela. The hotels offer a variety of activities that take up much of the space, including beach volleyball, spaghetti-eating contests, merengue lessons, parasailing and group aerobics. All of this plus the numerous local souvenir vendors and hair braiders makes for a frenetic scene, but there are still places reserved for tranquil sun worship. It's standard practice here to reserve a beach chair or a spot near the swimming pools by laying down your towel, so best follow suit early in the morning if you want a prime spot.

Even if you're not staying at Playa Dorada, getting through the front gate should be no problem; choose either from the two easy points of sneak entry onto the beach, one beside the *Dorada Naco* complex and the other just east of the *Playa Dorada Hotel*, or from the array of day passes (US$45–60) available from each resort, entitling you to five hours on

the grounds, including meals and drinks.

Costa Dorada

1km east of Puerto Plata. The newly built Costa Dorada, within walking distance of Puerto Plata, is an off-shoot of Playa Dorada that shares the same excellent beach but seeks to build a bridge between the walled-off all-inclusive complexes and the thriving urban community next door. The two Costa Dorada hotels make great alternatives to their Playa Dorada neighbours for those who plan to foray into the city because the quality here is excellent, the resorts quiet and secure, and the beaches lovely.

Costambar

1km west of Puerto Plata on the C-5. This rambling settlement consists of townhouses and private homes, time-shared, rented or owned by expats and well-to-do Dominicans. Once you make your way through a spaghetti bowl of ever-curling lanes, you'll find a lightly populated beach far better than the one in Puerto Plata (though obviously inferior to Playa Dorada), but it offers little shade. A couple of restaurants sit right on the water offering pizza and sandwiches, and views across the harbour of the city lights are an added bonus at night.

▲ CABLE CAR RIDE UP MOUNT ISABELA

▲ GROUP AEROBICS IN PLAYA DORADA

Hispaniolan parakeets, parrots and toucans. Admission includes a free lunch – though consider yourself warned that the food is pretty awful.

Playa Cofresí

5km west of Puerto Plata. Once backed by a small fishing village but now home to the deluxe *Hacienda* resort, Cofresí is one of the most stunning beaches on the island, and a major day-trip destination for Dominicans all across the island. The ocean here gets extremely choppy, though, so it's really better for bodysurfing and boogie-boarding than a pleasant swim. Along the beach you'll find a few shacks that serve delicious fried fish with *tostones* and beer for as little as US$4.

Ocean World

Western end of Playa Cofresí ☎291-1000, ⓦwww.ocean-world.info. Daily 9.30am–6pm. Admission US$55, US$40 for small children; US$35–120 to swim with dolphins, sea lions and nurse sharks. Discover the island's flourishing underwater world at this first-class ocean park with marine habitats teeming with dolphins, sharks, piranhas, snow leopards, toucans, stingrays and sea lions. The ambitious US$25-million park, modeled on the great ocean-life centres in Florida, also features massive tanks for snorkelling over an artificial reef swarming with colourful tropical fish and a superb viewing aquarium of piranhas. Large aviaries are aflutter with

Damajagua Cascades

20km southwest of Puerto Plata. This stunning series of cascades lie along the Río Damajagua. If you're driving, head down the C-5 toward Santiago until you see the Damajagua sign a kilometre south of the Texaco station in the town of Imbert. From there a dirt road leads east for a half-kilometre to a parking area, from where you'll be pointed in the direction of the cascades, which are a half-hour's hike further on. Twenty-three pretty, boulder-strewn waterfalls snake down the side of a mountain wilderness, the water crashing down at a breakneck pace. You'll also come across several crystal-clear swimming holes scattered along the way. It's a challenging but safe climb up, with a great hilltop view at the end. As little as five years ago, almost no one came here, but it's become quite a popular stopoff for the all-inclusive tour operators, and recently the local Peace Corps volunteer upgraded the quality of the trail, making the place a lot less chaotic.

Accommodation

Casa Colonial

Playa Dorada ☎320-2111, ⓕ320-2112, ⓦwww.victoriahoteles.com.do. This brand spanking new small hotel – which doesn't do all-inclusive or cheap package deals – has upped the ante for all accommodation in the area. A high-end haven, this luxury resort features large, beautiful, well-decorated rooms with facilities to match, including a mammoth pool, a glassed-in rooftop Jacuzzi with an ocean view, the best spa facilities in the area, high-speed Internet access in the rooms, wireless hotspot in the lobby, 24-hour room service, and on and on. US$120–200, depending on room size and view.

Gran Ventana

Playa Dorada ☎320-2111, ℻320-2112, ⊛www.victoriahoteles.com .do. One of the very best Playa Dorada resorts, though there is the occasional water-pressure problem in the bathrooms. The grounds are absolutely gorgeous, with tropical gardens, Baroque fountains and a meticulously groomed beach, plus extensive sports and impeccable service. In addition to the buffets, you can reserve a table at the top-notch *Octopus* seafood restaurant (guests only). US$100–155.

Iberostar Costa Dorada

Costa Dorada ☎320-1550 or 1000, ℻320-2023, ⊛www.iberostar.com. This relative newcomer is a good option with easy access to both Playa Dorada and Puerto Plata. It's also among the best in terms of quality – surprisingly good buffet food, standard amenities, well-manicured gardens and comfortable rooms. The lobby area can be noisy and chaotic, so request a room in the 7000 block, which is shielded from the disco noise but still has good views from the balconies. The à la carte restaurants are also above average, including a Brazilian steakhouse and a Mexican joint that offers a free margarita. Men are required to wear long pants and long sleeves for dinner at the à la carte restaurants, so don't just pack T-shirts and shorts. US$95–125.

Inter Clubs Fun Royale/Fun Tropicale

Playa Dorada ☎320-4054, ℻320-5301, ⊛www.funroyale-tropicale.com. Two adjacent resorts under a common, Dominican ownership. There's a leaning towards family vacations here with childcare facilities and plenty going on to entertain kids of all ages. The *Royale* has slightly larger rooms though not all come with balconies. The resorts share the pool areas and restaurants, which certainly adds to the variety, but most of the latter do need to be booked in advance. US$75–95.

Jack Tar Village

Playa Dorada ☎320-3800, ℻320-4161, ⊛www.occidentalhotels.com.

▼ CLIMBING DAMAJAGUA CASCADES

The oldest and still one of the most highly regarded of the Playa Dorada resorts, though it's under new management and service isn't what it used to be. Still not bad, considering the two large swimming pools, one with hot tub. The rooms are rather characterless but well appointed. For each week you stay here, you're entitled to eat once at each of the à la carte restaurants, which specialize in Caribbean, Italian and seafood respectively. They also have the best casino in Playa Dorada. US$105–155.

Lomar

Puerto Plata Malecón, just west of Puerto Plata Beach ☎320-8555. One of the best options in town for its clean rooms, relatively high level of comfort, cable TV, generator, a/c, mini-fridge and plenty of hot water. The staff here is simply awesome, and this is a great deal. US$25–35.

Marien Coral Hilton

Costa Dorada ☎320-1010, ℻320-1414, ⊛www.coralbyhilton.com. A new Costa Dorada property that's a bit less noisy than the *Iberostar* resort next door, with top-notch service, nice pool area, spacious rooms with great water pressure and a variety of standard amenities, and easy access to Puerto Plata. One of the area's best choices. US$95–110.

Occidental Playa Dorada

Playa Dorada ☎320-3988, ℻320-1190, ⊛www.occidental-hoteles .com. Three-storey hotel with great sea views and an appealing choice of restaurants, especially the gourmet *La Palma*. Full watersports package and a great pool to relax by as well. US$100–135.

Paradise Resort

Playa Dorada ☎320-3663, ℻320-4858, ⊛www.amhsamarina.com. Known for their excellent restaurants (especially *Michelangelo*), sports facilities and children's programme. The rooms and grounds are in perfect condition, and ethnic "theme nights" like Mexican, Chinese and Italian keep the buffet food varied. This is the closest hotel to the beach and it's very popular with British vacationers. US$105–140.

Portofino

Av Hermanas Mirabal just off the Malecón, Puerto Plata ☎586-2858, ℻586-5050. Clean and comfortable air-conditioned rooms, way nicer and quieter than the nearby competition for only a few dollars more. US$25–35.

Puerto Plata Beach

Puerto Plata Malecón, just west of Av Hermanas Mirabal ☎586-4243. Formerly an all-inclusive beach resort, they offer extremely comfortable rooms and full-service apartments for a rock-bottom price. The only problem is that they don't have a generator for the rooms, which means you may be stuck in darkness for a few hours each night. US$25–35.

Puerto Plata Village

Playa Dorada ☎320-4012, ℻320-5113, ⊛www.puertoplatavillage .com. For those who want to escape some of the frenzy of Playa Dorada, try this large, quiet compound of cottages, supposedly based upon the town of Puerto Plata itself. The hotel grounds are a bit worn, but the rooms are clean and well maintained, if a little tacky. It's a long walk from the beach but there's unlimited nonmotorized watersports when you do get there and it's right by the golf course. In addition to the decent buffet food, guests can dine free at an excellent beachfront pizzeria. No children's programme, though. US$75–125.

Sofy's Bed and Breakfast

Puerto Plata, Las Rosas 3 and Ginebra ☎ & ℻ 586-6411, ✉ gillin.n@verizon .net.do. A cozy private home with a hibiscus-filled courtyard patio and two large rooms. Price includes free laundry service and a terrific breakfast, including pancakes, eggs, Canadian bacon, fresh fruit and coffee. US$35–40.

Restaurants

Aguaceros

Puerto Plata Malecón 32. Dominican dishes served in a festive, oceanfront barn. The *lambí* and other seafood dishes are reasonably priced and as good as in the more expensive restaurants.

Barco's

Puerto Plata Malecón 6. A great people-watching spot on the Malecón with a sidewalk patio and a second-floor terrace. They serve tasty pizzas, lamb and goat dishes, along with steak *criolla* and grilled dorada.

Buddy's

Costambar, Almirante 11. A Costambar institution and gathering point for the local expat community. Basically a standard burger and seafood joint in an outdoor patio a block from the beach, but an amiable place to spend an hour between sun-worshipping sessions.

Cafe Cito

Costa Dorada, Sosúa Highway Km 4, opposite the Costa Dorada Resort. The best restaurant in town, where you can tuck into great food – try the filet mignon or the curried chicken for around RD$200–350 – to the pleasant accompaniment of jazz or blues. It's run by the local Canadian honorary consul, who is a good contact for local

▲ CAFE CITO

information and a generally interesting character. Eat here on Wednesdays and get half off the next meal.

Chris & Mady's

Calle Cofresí, Cofresí ☎970-7052. Located on the same road that leads to Ocean World and the *Hacienda* resort, this open-air beachfront sports bar serves quality burgers, seafood (grilled *mahi mahi* is a house speciality) and pizza for around RD$200 per person.

Jamvi's

Puerto Plata, Malecón 18. Clean and efficient pizza joint right by the beach with a children's playground and a terrace above where you can watch the world go by. A pie runs around RD$200.

Jardín Suizo

Puerto Plata, Malecón 13 ☎586-9564. Top-end international fare in a smart but relaxed building close to the water's edge. The RD$200 seafood specials include excellent seared tuna steaks, which go well with an ice-cold Presidente beer.

Papillon

Villas Cofresí, Cofresí ☎970-7640. Relatively formal French-leaning restaurant across the highway from Playa Cofresí, with a host of terrific seafood dishes. The quiet, candlelit ambience is one of the best in the area, and the chef really knows what he's doing. The RD$200 Sunday brunches here are an excellent bargain.

Polanco

Puerto Plata, Beller 60. Quality budget Dominican fare plus pizza and burgers, served in an open-air enclosure near the Parque Central. Also a good spot for breakfast.

El Portal

Costambar, at the Costambar Gate, the main village entrance. Excellent home-cooked Dominican fare in a thatch-roofed patio setting. The fish is tender and fresh, and the *sancocho* and *mofongo* are sublime.

Roma II

Puerto Plata, Beller 43 ☎586-8358. Tasty international food with RD$250 Italian dishes dominating the menu. The lasagna is spot-on and there are plenty of seafood choices too. One of the smartest options in town, so best to book ahead.

Bars

Cafe Cíto

Costa Dorada, Sosúa Highway Km 4. You're more likely to hear Billie Holiday or Charlie Parker than merengue or bachata in this ambient spot. They serve the best mixed drinks in town, including positively addictive "rum mudslides". Live blues on Thursday nights.

El Carey Beach Bar

Costambar, west end of Costambar beach. A bustling lunch spot on the beach, good for burgers, soft-shell tacos and grilled fish. They've also got a hammock where you can relax oceanside while sipping your tropical drink.

Hemingway's Bar and Grill

Playa Dorada, Plaza Playa Dorada. Haven for crazed drunken tourists intent on having a good time. Friday's ear-splitting karaoke night is the most popular; Thursdays and Saturdays feature a good rock'n'roll band. The food is good but expensive.

Nelly's

Puerto Plata, Av Hermanas Mirabal and Malecón. Amiable, Swiss-run outdoor bar with a bustling oceanfront location.

Sam's Bar and Grill

Puerto Plata, Ariza 34. Pleasantly divey, established meeting place for fellow travellers, with good-value daily food specials and a range of drinks. Set in a ramshackle nineteenth-century hotel space and packed with American and British expats at all hours. The Philly cheesesteak, made with filet mignon, is highly recommended. American breakfasts served as well, and they offer Internet access for US$3 an hour.

TJ's Canadian Bar

Puerto Plata, Av Hermanas Mirabal and Malecón. Major hang-out for an older Canadian expat crowd and a nice place to stop off for a beer and a burger.

Clubs and entertainment

La Barrica

Puerto Plata, Circunvalación Sur 35 and Av Colón. Hip, strictly Dominican music disco catering mostly to indigenous city-dwellers cutting vicious moves. There are no lights in the entire club – the waiters use flashlights. The standard drink order is Cuba libre servicio: two cokes, one bottle of dark rum and a pitcher of ice.

Crazy Moon

Playa Dorada, Paradise Resort. Cover US$1–4. Dark, purple-neon nightclub mixing the occasional merengue with a healthy dose of techno and pop. Something of a tourist meat-market, as it draws crowds from all of the surrounding resorts. Closed Sun.

Fun Tropicale

Hotel Fun Tropicale, Playa Dorada. An exceptionally fun hotel disco that features live music most nights of the week – a big improvement over the minor-league Las Vegas floor shows prevalent in the other resorts.

Ojilvis

Av Colón, just south of Circunvalación Sur, Puerto Plata. Typical "car wash"-style Dominican dance hall, frequented mostly by locals though it does see limited tourist traffic. Earplugs might be a good idea, but it does give you a great sense of what the local nightlife is all about. Great for dancing, though the space is unbelievably crowded.

Orión

Puerto Plata, 30 de Marzo and 12 de Julio. The largest and most popular dance spot in town, though it's a little intimidating for tourists, featuring strictly merengue and bachata. Whenever the major local acts come to town, they usually perform here.

▲ HEMINGWAY'S BAR AND GRILL

The Northwest Coast

West of Puerto Plata lie a series of remote pueblos linked by unpaved roads, where campesinos live much as they have for the last five centuries. If you truly want to get away from it all, visit this unspoilt region: in place of the paved highways, resort complexes and golf courses that prevail on the Northeast Coast, here you'll find vast stretches of small family farms and an untrammelled wilderness unfolding along rough dirt tracks. Fine coral reefs remain intact between Punta Rucia and Monte Cristi, while lovely coastal detours include the seaside village of Luperón; scenic El Castillo, which holds the remains of Columbus's first settlement, La Isabela; and the twin beaches Playa Ensenata and Punta Rucia – as beautiful as any on the island. Monte Cristi is also worth considering, as it's bordered by two large national parks and a series of small desert islands.

Imbert and Guzmancito

Two routes lead from Puerto Plata to Luperón, the first – and quicker – being the Carretera Luperón, which you can pick up 1km north of Imbert, a town marked by its large Texaco station. The second route from Puerto Plata to Luperón is a much rougher ride, but offers better scenery and an intimate look at the island's rural peasantry, or campesinos, as you drive through a series of seaside campos – outposts so small they couldn't even be called pueblos – dotted with thatch huts, small vegetable gardens and freely roaming farm animals. From the Carretera Puerto Plata, take the northwest turnoff marked "Guzmancito", 10km beyond Puerto Plata. Just after turning, you'll hit the small beach of **Playa Maimón**, which typically has a smattering of locals. You're better off forging on to **Playa Guzmancito**, a

Getting there and getting around

Getting around the northwest is more of a challenge than the rest of the northern coast but not impossible. Caribe Tours is the only major bus company that services the Northwest Coast, and only goes to Monte Cristi and Luperón. The Carretera 5 veers south just west of Puerto Plata, making it more of a challenge to head further west by car because most of the roads are of poor quality. From the Carretera Puerto Plata that heads south towards Santiago, you'll find a number of turnoffs leading successively to Guzmancito, Luperón, La Isabela and Punta Rucia, hellish pot-holed moonscapes for the most part, but slowly in the process of being paved. The only one that's easily accessible now is the Carretera Luperón that veers off from the Carretera 5 near Imbert and heads all the way through Luperón to El Castillo and Parque Nacional La Isabela. Guaguas run along each of these roads during the day. Beyond Punta Rucia are mule tracks; you'll have to head south to the Carretera Duarte that stretches along the western Cibao Valley to reach Monte Cristi.

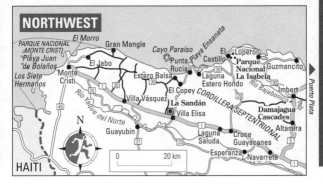

gorgeous, mostly abandoned beach another 10km down the road near the tiny fishing campo Cruce de Guzmán, where you can camp if you ask permission from the townsfolk first. From here the road passes through the foothills of the Cordillera Septentrional for 15km, affording spectacular ocean views before ending at La Sabana on the Carretera Luperón.

Luperón

40km west of Puerto Plata. Despite being the most developed of the western beach towns, with a popular all-inclusive resort and a large marina along its outskirts, Luperón maintains a dusty, low-key feel, and there is precious little to see or do in the town itself.

The action, as usual, is along the beach, **Playa Grande**, a kilometre of sand lined with sea grapes and palms. It's not too far off the main road, the Carretera de las Américas, which has a couple of restaurants good for lunch or a drink.

Puerto Blanca Marina

Half a kilometre west of Luperón. This lively mooring spot serves as a great social centre for expats in the area, including famous sailor Bruce Van Sant, whose *Gentleman's Guide to Passages South* is a bible for those doing the tricky "thorny path" between Florida and Anguilla. The bay here is the best place to rest from the trade winds, and is thus usually bustling with numerous world-travelling vagabonds making the most of the ample protection from hurricanes and tropical storms; as a result, you can usually find someone willing to take you on a sailboat day-trip to the

▲ LUPERÓN MARINA

▲ EL CASTILLO

hard-to-reach reefs around La Isabela and Punta Rucia. A trip costs around US$100. Ask for a recommendation from Lenin, the proprietor of the marina.

El Castillo

13km west of Luperón on Carretera de las Américas. The sleepy seaside village of El Castillo sits on the site of Columbus's first permanent settlement, the remains of which are now nestled inside the small Parque Nacional La Isabela just east of the village. Set on a splendid bay of tranquil, blue water and a solid wall of imposing, Olympian peaks stretching in both directions, it's easy to see why Columbus set up shop in El Castillo. The village itself consists of just a few houses scattered around a grid of tiny dirt roads on a steep hill – but visitors come for the scenery and peace and quiet rather than the excitement.

Playa Isabela, a couple of metres down a marked dirt path just right of *Rancho del Sol* (see p.128), attracts few beachgoers and instead has just a couple of small wooden boats moored offshore and children fishing at the water's edge. The placid atmosphere is interrupted daily at around 2pm by the *Kon Tiki* party boat that comes here from *Luperón Beach Resort*, blasting steel-drum music. If you have a 4WD you can head about twenty minutes east along the water and through a patch of high grass to a wilderness beach that won't have a single other person on it.

A kilometre offshore from El Castillo is an intact, living **coral reef** – rare in the Dominican Republic – where you can explore a healthy, multicoloured reef bed that's home to thousands of tropical fish and sea creatures. *Rancho del Sol* (see p.128) arranges regular scuba and snorkelling trips, and can also take you to other remote reefs west of Punta Rucia.

Parque Nacional La Isabela

Park entrance is just off the main highway, before you reach El Castillo. Mon–Sat 9am–5.30pm. RD$40. The ruins of the first European town in the New World, La Isabela, lie within this national park, centred on the private home of Columbus, perched atop a prominent ocean bluff. The rest of the park encompasses the town's excavated stone foundations and a small museum, though to see either you'll need to hire a local guide from the main park

123

PLACES The Northwest Coast

office (RD$100 tip). You'll see two large warehouses, a sentry tower, a chapel and Columbus's house, which retains a good portion of its walls intact. A number of skeletons have been unearthed from the chapel's cemetery; one – a Spaniard who died of malaria – is rather unceremoniously on display in a box near the museum.

The museum itself offers an account of the cultures of both Spaniards and Tainos at the time of their first encounter. Better than the solemn recitations by the guide are the hundreds of excavated artefacts, including a pottery oven, a kiln and several containers that still held mercury (used to purify gold) when they were unearthed, along with smaller items such as a tiny sixteenth-century crucifix, unglazed Moorish-style pottery shards and several Taino religious icons.

Templo de las Américas
Across the main highway from Parque Nacional La Isabela. Daily 8.30am–5pm. Templo de las Américas, a spotless neo-colonial church topped by a high central dome, was constructed for Pope John

Paul II's visit to La Isabela in 1992 for the Columbus Centenary. The pope gave Mass there on the anniversary of the admiral's landing; a plaque commemorates the visit. The interior is simple but striking, with marble floors and red-brick walls; even better is the elevated vista of Bahía de Isabela from the top of the steps.

Laguna Estero Hondo
9km west of El Castillo. Laguna Estero Hondo is one of the last remaining Dominican homes of the manatee, which has been killed off in droves in recent decades by destruction of habitat and speedboat accidents. Paraíso Tours (℡612-8499) in Punta Rucia can organize boat excursions into the lagoon though it may be best to give them a few days' notice; a short trip to the lagoon is included in their boat trip to Cayo Paraíso. Even then, sightings are not guaranteed, but you will see a gorgeous mangrove preserve that serves as a haven for tropical birds, such as egrets, wood storks and roseate spoonbills.

▲ LA ISABELA RUINS

Playa El Pato, Playa Ensenada and Punta Rucia

From El Castillo the road to Punta Rucia extends west around the lagoon and heads through increasingly arid scrubland to a series of beaches that relatively few foreign visitors make it to. Though the road is graded, it's mainly dirt and there are two shallow rivers for which bridges have yet to be built. It's usually possible to drive through these and there's never a shortage of locals loitering nearby to assist you if you're not confident. After 13km lies the sparsely populated Playa El Pato, a small cove protected by a giant reef that turns it into a large natural swimming pool. The more popular Playa Ensenada, 1km west, draws Dominican families who come to splash about in its shallow waters. The western end of the kilometre-long beach, where it meets the road, is quieter, with stunning white sand, gently lapping turquoise water and a few small boats bobbing just offshore, the mountains looming in the background. The eastern end of the beach promises a totally different cultural experience, with radios blasting bachata and shacks selling tasty food and inexpensive rum.

Just around the point from Playa Ensenada, Punta Rucia is arguably the most beautiful beach on the north coast, with more bone-white sand and great mountain views. It attracts fewer people than Ensenada but has several informal local places to stop for lunch or a beer, some with live music. The small point that separates the two beaches is bordered by a thriving coral reef, which offers good snorkelling.

Cayo Paraíso

7km west of Punta Rucia. Boat tours head from Punta Rucia (and from some Puerto Plata–based hotels) to Cayo Paraíso, a small, perfectly circular desert island surrounded by thriving coral and sealife and with a palm-thatched restaurant in its centre. The company that runs the trips is Punta Rucia–based Paraíso Tours (☎612-8499 or 970-7606, ⓦwww.cayoparaiso.com; US$30); in addition to snorkelling and a big lunch, you'll head through the brackish Laguna Estero Hondo on the way back, past dense snarls of mangroves and perhaps even a manatee or two.

Carretera Duarte

Borders the Cordillera Septentrional to the south. Carretera Duarte provides a far easier way to reach Monte Cristi than the coastal mule tracks. The well-paved freeway stretches from Santiago

▲ BOAT TOUR TO CAYO PARAÍSO

to Monte Cristi, intersecting the Carretera Puerto Plata at Navarrete, a major tobacco centre. As you move west, tobacco fields give way to banana trees and rice paddies, and at Villa Elisa, the land suddenly becomes arid, transforming into a cactus-dominated desert teeming with goats. The towns that line it are all fairly basic, with at most a couple of *colmados* and the occasional cockfighting arena, and none are advisable for stopping off, except perhaps **Laguna Saluda**, 20km west of Navarrete, with two no-frills accommodations if you need a bed for the night.

▲ MONTE CRISTI CARNIVAL

Monte Cristi

140km west of Puerto Plata. Monte Cristi has the feel of the mythic Wild West, a dusty frontier town bearing the occasional tarnished remnant of its opulent past along wide, American-style boulevards that the sand incessantly tries to reclaim. Founded in 1501, it's one of the oldest European cities in the New World, and became an important port in the eighteenth century, shipping out vast quantities of mahogany. The town's prosperity came to an abrupt end after Trujillo shut down its shipping in retribution for local resistance to his rule.

The only remaining industry of note comes from the large Morton saltpans – rectangular pools of the salty local water that are filled from a canal and then harvested by allowing the water to evaporate – just north and south of the city, which supply much of North America's table salt. There are a couple of century-old mansions worth seeing in town, but most people use Monte Cristi as a base from which to explore the local beaches and the Parque Nacional Monte Cristi. Within town, the charming Parque Central is worth a look, with a singular Eiffel-style clock tower, imported from France

Carnival in Monte Cristi

Monte Cristi is somewhat infamous for its peculiarly violent Carnival celebrations. Each Sunday in February, the locals split into two groups: the **Toros**, who dress in stylized Carnival bull masks and bright cloth outfits decorated with mirrors, whistles and other miscellaneous bangles, and the unadorned **Civilis**. Both parties protect themselves by putting on four or five layers of clothing, including winter coats, then proceed to attack each other in the streets with bullwhips. Onlookers are supposed to be safe from the proceedings, but with hundreds of people whizzing deadly weapons through the air, you're better off watching the "festivities" from the second-floor balcony of the *Hotel Chic* restaurant, conveniently located in the centre of the action.

at the turn of the century, and a pretty faux-colonial church across the street. Also at the park on Duarte is the Victorian Villa Doña Emilia Jiménez, a palatial old building that was the residence of an early Dominican president and until recently served as the town courthouse. Just south of the park sit several gingerbread homes, including one on Calle Mella that was owned by Cuban liberator Máximo Gómez. It's now a fairly dreary museum (Mon–Fri 9am–noon & 2.30–5.30pm; free), set in a nice garden, with period furnishings, personal mementoes, and an account of his fight for the liberation of both Cuba and the Dominican Republic from Spain.

Playa Juan de Bolaños and Playa de los Muertos

Just north of Monte Cristi, 2km north on Calle Bolaños past the saltpans.
The soothing Playa Juan de Bolaños has a cluster of restaurants at its entrance, but elsewhere it's undeveloped, and the stark desert whiteness of the landscape makes the water's perfect turquoise even more inviting. East of the restaurants, the beach road passes numerous

small fishing boats and the large *Club Nautico Marina* before arriving at the entrance to the eastern half of Parque Nacional Monte Cristi. A half-kilometre to the west is a river you'll have to ford by foot to reach the beach known locally as Playa de los Muertos (Beach of the Dead), its most notable feature the palm trees that have been uprooted and deposited here by tide and tropical storms.

Parque Nacional Monte Cristi

2km west of Monte Cristi at the eastern end of Playa Bolaños. RD$50.
The park protects the towering El Morro mesa, an enormous river delta with a wildlife-filled mangrove coast and a series of seven nearby islands known as **Los Siete Hermanos**, coral-reef-wreathed sand protrusions that sea turtles use to lay their eggs. To explore the mangroves and islands, try hiring a fishing boat at Playa Bolaños (from RD$600 per person), or a small yacht at the Playa Bolaños marina (from RD$1500 per person).

The park is essentially divided into two parts by Monte Cristi's beaches. The eastern section is often referred to as Parque El

▼ PLAYA JUAN DE BOLAÑOS

Morro, after the flat-topped mesa that takes up a good chunk of it. At the foot of El Morro's eastern slope is a lovely and unpopulated beach but unfortunately, the water's a little rough for swimming. From here you can rent a boat to **Isla Cabrita**, some 300m offshore, a large island punctuated by a lighthouse and with a beautiful beach, **Playa El Cayo**. The waters surrounding the park contain several shipwrecks, two of them colonial-era galleons.

The western half of the national park encompasses a rather uninteresting inland swath of arid desert environment and a far more beautiful dense mangrove coast dotted with small lagoons. The coast is accessible only by boat; informal tours are led from the *Los Jardines* hotel (RD$1000; see p.128), on which you'll see several river deltas thick with mangroves and perhaps a couple of crocodiles. The swamp is also home to innumerable orchids, along with ibises, egrets, pelicans and a host of other birds. The same hotel offers tours to Los Siete Hermanos, seven islands with arid vegetation and desolate beaches. By far the most attractive is known as "Tuna", in honour of the gorgeous, white-flowering tuna cacti that grow here.

Accommodation

Casa del Sol

Carretera Isabela between the town and marina, Luperón ☎ & ℻571-8403. Best of the Luperón-area budget options, this small, family-run operation offers a few decent rooms above a local restaurant. Nothing special, but the place is kept clean, has a view of the ocean, and the downstairs restaurant is actually quite good. US$15.

Casa Van Sant

Luperón ☎571-8690 or 486-4410, ✉rosavansant@yahoo.com. If you're staying in town for a few days, you can rent a full-service apartment in this large house, majestically located on top of a hill that looks out over the bay and marina. The well-kept apartment has hot water and a kitchen stocked with all the necessary utensils. It's owned by a famous Caribbean yachtsman. US$25.

Cayo Arena

Playa Juan de Bolaños, 250m west of the beach entrance, Monte Cristi ☎579-3145, ℻579-2096, ⓦwww.cayoarena.com. The most luxurious hotel in Monte Cristi boasts large, full-service apartments right on the beach, with ocean-view balconies, a/c, kitchenettes, swimming pool, bar and 24-hour security. The apartments sleep six and are ideal for a family. They also run local tours, including deep-sea fishing (US$70–700, depending on the length of time), snorkelling on one of the Siete Hermanos (US$50), organized hikes up El Morro (US$20) and kayaking trips to the lagoons around Manzanillo (US$20). US$35–50.

Hotel Dally

Calle Duarte at the Parque Central, Luperón ☎571-8034. Small, somewhat spartan rooms that are clean and comfortable if not particularly exciting, with private cold-water showers and satellite TV. A smart restaurant serves inexpensive seafood, much of it caught locally. US$18.

Los Jardines

26 San Fernando at Playa Juan de Bolaños, Monte Cristi ☎579-2091, ⓦwww.elbistrot.com. A little more basic than *Cayo Arena*, but a better value if you're travelling alone or with one other. Simple beachfront rooms with cold-water showers – good for those seeking simplicity, sea views and access to the hotel's comprehensive set of reasonably priced local tours, including boat trips to the mangrove lagoons in Manzanillo (US$25) and across the border to Haiti's Fort Liberte. They also rent bicycles, rowboats and jeeps. US$30–40.

Luperón Beach Resort

Carretera Isabela at the town's western entrance, Luperón ☎571-8303, ⓕ571-8180. A high-quality all-inclusive resort that's easily the equal of what you might find in Playa Dorada. Very comfortable, modern rooms, many of them overlooking the ocean. The pretty, rambling grounds encompass a large swimming pool, a spa and a decent buffet restaurant. You can partake in a number of activities, including horseback riding and watersports. The beach here is truly stunning, but expect a lot of local vendors trying to sell you souvenirs as you sun worship. US$80–125.

Miamar

El Castillo ⓕ471-9157, no telephone. Set high on the hill above town with stunning views over the bay, this well-constructed little hotel offers large rooms with great views, private balconies, king-sized beds and cold-water showers, but is a bit run down due to lack of business. A couple of rooms have kitchenettes, and there's a swimming pool, bar and good restaurant. US$25–35.

Punta Rucia Sol

Punta Rucia. Quite the hidden – albeit basic – gem, this place oozes a timeless, unhurried tranquillity that's quite addictive. Sadly, the owner is here only about half the time since her husband died, so you simply have to show up and see if she's around. US$20.

Rancho del Sol

Carretera Isabela at the town entrance, El Castillo ☎696-0325. Simple but well-maintained waterfront duplexes with kitchen and private bath. Two have a/c, and breakfast is included in the price. They also own a speedboat and catamaran for private fishing, snorkelling and water-skiing tours (around RD$800 for a half day). US$50.

San Fernando

Playa Juan de Bolaños, Parque Nacional Monte Cristi. No phone. High-quality budget accommodation right at the base of the El Morro mesa, as pretty a spot as you'll find in this entire region. Spacious cabañas with great views, comfortable beds, cold-water showers and mosquito nets. They also have a little fish restaurant and bar attached. A great bargain for those who want to be surrounded by majestic scenery and don't need amenities like a/c or TV. US$25–30.

Restaurants

Cocomar

Playa Juan de Bolaños, Monte Cristi. By far the best of the budget beachfront seafood restaurants, with unbelievably good kingfish and crab dishes starting at around RD$150. The concrete floor and shuttered windows can feel quite sombre when it's quiet, but an amiable crowd usually keeps it lively.

Demaris

Punta Rucia. Small, homely open-air restaurant, with tasty traditional Dominican seafood, though they're periodically inundated with package boat tours, to whom they serve low-quality buffet food.

Le Bistrot

26 San Fernando at Playa Juan de Bolaños, Monte Cristi. Casual, friendly beach eatery featuring outstanding fresh seafood, with specialities like octopus salad (that tastes similar to ceviche), heaping platters of salted shrimp and barbecued creole-style goat.

Louisa's Chicken Shack

Calle Duarte just north of Parque Central, Luperón. Terrific, artery-clogging fried chicken and fish in a small, unmarked blue building in the centre of town. Sides include *tostones*, baked bananas, beans and rice and french fries.

Milagro's

Just off the beach near Rancho del Sol, El Castillo. A small, friendly comedor, with a good selection of local dishes including excellent piquant goat, and fish catch of the day – fried, grilled or *criolla*.

La Sandán

Carretera Duarte at the entrance to Punta Rucia, Villa Elisa. One of the country's most famous restaurants with a big concrete outdoor patio where they serve deliciously spiced creole goat, as well as chicken-and-rice and other traditional campesino favourites.

Clubs and entertainment

Hotel Chic

Parque Central, Monte Cristi. *Hotel Chic* features an unbelievably loud disco that's been around forever and still draws in big crowds, though these days it's not as hip as *Oceania*. Check it out anyway to see what a traditionally garish, mirror-filled Dominican disco is all about.

Luperón Marina

Luperón. A lively place most nights of the week – especially if there are a good number of boats anchored at bay – as it's the centre of various sailing-community activities. Happy hour daily from 5 to 7pm, film showings on Wednesday nights, pot luck dinners on Monday, Wednesday and Friday, and a flea market on Sunday afternoons.

Luperón Parque Central

Luperón. The main festive area in town, with two discos on opposite ends of the park and crowds of people hanging out and playing music from boom boxes all along the street. Especially popular during the town's frequent blackouts.

Oceania

Monte Cristi. Best dance hall in Monte Cristi, set just off the beach and much more modern than you would expect way out in the middle of nowhere – still plays mostly merengue, though. They also have a casual café for sitting down and sipping a tropical drink as you look out over the stark expanse of El Morro, the deep blue sea and the stars.

Santiago and around

A vibrant provincial city known worldwide for its first-class cigars, Santiago serves as the chief transport point for Cibao tobacco, bananas, coffee and chocolate. Set at the intersection of the western Cibao and the Vega Real, and with easy access to the country's north and south ports, Santiago's prime location has brought settlers back time and again – its population of 800,000 trails only that of Santo Domingo. For visitors, the main draw is the buzzing nightlife, tobacco factories and magnificent new cultural centre and museum Centro León Jimenes. Outside the city lies beautiful mountain scenery and the opportunity to rub shoulders with locals away from the traditional tourist trail. Consider a short jaunt to San José de las Matas, a pretty village in the northern foothills of the Cordillera Central, only a half hour from the city.

▲ MONUMENTO A LOS HÉROES DE LAS RESTAURACIÓN

Monumento a los Héroes de la Restauración

Av Francia and Calle del Sol. Mon–Sat 9am–noon 2–5pm. Free. Santiago's most impressive sight, built by Trujillo in honour of himself, was quickly rededicated upon his death to the soldiers who lost their lives in the War of Independence with Spain. A

Getting there and getting around

The new Cibao International Airport (☎582-7179) is just a twenty-minute drive from the city, but you're more likely to be arriving by land, and all three highway entrances to town – the Autopista Duarte, the Carretera Duarte and the Carretera Turística – lead directly to the city centre. Several bus companies service Santiago, including Caribe Tours (☎576-0790) on 27 de Febrero and Las Américas, Metro Tours (☎582-9111) on JP Duarte and Maimón, Terra Bus (☎587-3000) on Avenida Francia and Del Sol, and Espinal (☎575-7619) on 27 de Febrero and Libertad. There are also guagua stations on the corner of 30 de Marzo and Cucurullo (guaguas to Mao and Monción), and on Calle Valerio a block west of Parque Valerio (to San José de las Matas).

Cibao tobacco

Tobacco was first cultivated (and given its name) by the Tainos, who pressed the leafy plant into a rock-hard substance to be smoked in pipes. Many Cibao peasants still make this form of tobacco – called *andullo* – which you can find if you ask around in Tamboril, Navarrete or Villa González; it's sometimes even for sale in local *colmados*. Export began in 1679, when Cibao farmers started growing it for the French colony on the western side of the island. For two centuries, Dominican tobacco was widely praised as top quality, but when large-scale export to Germany for cigarette filler began in the mid-nineteenth century, that quality began to erode.

Nevertheless, the best Dominican cigars are made from Cibao tobacco, and you can purchase some of the regional product while in town. You may not be able to find the most recognizable brands locally, but you'll find ones of similar quality.

statue of Victory personified as a woman tops its seventy-metre pillar, supported by a marble base, her arms extended martially towards the sky. Helped by its position atop a hill, the monument is visible from the entire city, something locals say was originally intended to symbolize the omnipresence of the secret police. You can climb the stairs to the top of the monument to take in a breathtaking panorama of Santiago and the surrounding valley and mountains.

Gran Teatro del Cibao

Just east of the monument. This palatial rectangle of Italian marble boasts a main auditorium that seats fifteen thousand and has near-perfect acoustics. Unfortunately, the majority of Santiago residents can't afford the hefty RD$500–750 ticket price, so the large hall goes mostly unused. The theatre hosts a couple of opera productions per year, with occasional merengue concerts, chamber music and theatre in the smaller concert hall.

Centro León Jimenes

27 de Febrero 146, just east of Av Estrella Sadhalá in Villa Progreso ☎582-2315, ✆www.centroleon.org

.do. Tues & Thurs–Sun 9am–6pm, Wed 9am–8pm. RD$50. One of Santiago's most compelling attractions, the multi-faceted Centro León Jimenes houses an amazing Dominican art collection, an equally remarkable exhibit of Taino artefacts, a cultural conference centre, a small film theatre and a mock tobacco factory set up like those from the turn of the twentieth century. Art highlights include local modernist masterpieces such as Jaime Colsón's folk-cubist *Hombre con Pipa* and Celeste Woss y Gil's imposing self-portrait *Autorretrato con Cigarillo*, as well as more abstract works, from Elvis Avilés' *El muro II* to Paul Guidicelli's

▼ SANTIAGO CIGARS

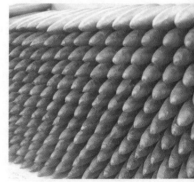

expressionist depiction of a *vodú* priest sacrificing a chicken, *Brujo disfrazado de pájaro*. The Taino collection includes a host of intact aboriginal necklaces, *cemi* statuettes, decorated pots, daggers, axheads and vomit sticks, which were used to induce vomiting after a large banquet. The early twentieth-century tobacco factory has cigars for sale (around RD$20 apiece), and you can also visit the modern Jimenes factory across the street as part of the admission price, where you can observe cigars being made on the assembly-room floor and sample a stogie in a plush smoking room.

Calle del Sol and Parque Duarte

Bustling Calle del Sol is the city's major shopping district, lined with department stores, banks and sidewalk stalls selling clothing, household wares and fast food. Follow it north to 30 de Marzo and you'll pass through the heart of the city before arriving at Parque Duarte, a bit overcrowded but covered by a tree canopy and lined with horse-and-carriage drivers giving rides to the monument and back; the price is negotiable, but expect to pay around RD$250.

At the park's southern end

▲ **1**, Puerto Plata & Monte Cristi

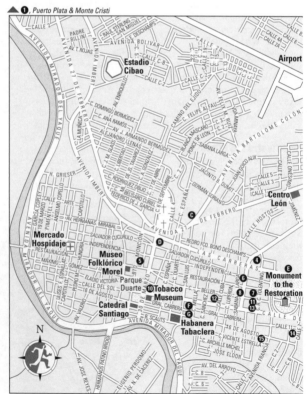

▼ S. José de las Matas

stands the 1895 **Catedral de Santiago**, a lavender concrete building with intricate carvings on its mahogany portals and stained-glass windows by contemporary Dominican artist Rincón Mora. The marble tomb of nineteenth-century dictator Ulises Heureaux is in the sanctuary. Just across the street is the excellent **Museo del Tabaco**, on 16 de Agosto and 30 de Marzo (Tues–Fri 9am– noon & 2–5pm, Sat 9am–noon; free), housed in an old Victorian tobacco warehouse. Exhibits cover the history of the crop's use dating back to Taino times, its social and economic impact

on the region and quick looks at various farming methods; you can also visit a mock cigar-room where tobacco is processed and rolled.

North of the park are two of downtown's more attractive buildings, the **Centro de Recreo** – an ornate mansion that looks more like a mosque – and the **Palacio Consistorial** (Tues–Fri 10am–noon & 2– 5.30pm, Sat & Sun 10am–2pm; free), a renovated gingerbread that was once city hall but now houses a small museum documenting Santiago's history, mostly through photographs. Around the corner sits the

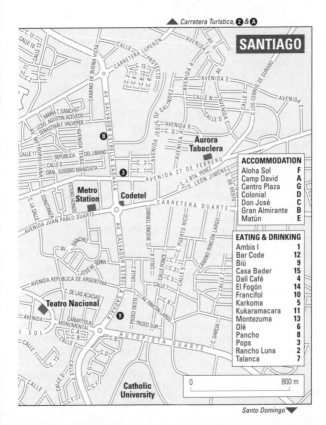

▲ Carretera Turística, ❷ & ⓐ

SANTIAGO

ACCOMMODATION

Aloha Sol	F
Camp David	A
Centro Plaza	G
Colonial	D
Don José	C
Gran Almirante	B
Matún	E

EATING & DRINKING

Ambis I	1
Bar Code	12
Biú	9
Casa Bader	15
Dalí Café	4
El Fogón	14
Francifol	10
Karkoma	5
Kukaramacara	11
Montezuma	13
Olé	6
Pancho	8
Pops	3
Rancho Luna	2
Talanca	7

0   800 m

Santo Domingo ▼

▲ MUSEO FOLKLÓRICO

nondescript **Centro de la Cultura**, home of the highly regarded School of Fine Arts and with regular opera, theatre and chamber music productions in its auditorium.

Museo Folklórico Tomás Morel

Restauración 174, a few blocks northwest of Parque Duarte ☎582-6787. Mon–Fri 9am–noon & 3–6pm. Free. The fascinating Museo Folklórico de Tomás Morel is somewhat misleadingly pitched as a house of horrors. The dilapidated condition of the exterior does nothing to alter this expectation, but inside you'll find a remarkable collection of papier-mâché carnival masks, alongside various Taino artefacts, and a faded sixteenth-century painting of the Virgin Mary. Hidden among the scattered exhibits are the Republic's first telephone, first television and even the first wood saw. There's also an accordion that once belonged

to Nico Lora, often thought of as the father of merengue. The masks, though, are the main focus, with an array of spectacularly baroque and evil-looking demons from La Vega, the simpler but no less malevolent Cimarrón *diablos* of Cabral, and several masks from politically oriented San Cristóbal – including one with a skin of American flags and nuclear missiles in place of bull horns.

Mercado Hospidaye

Western downtown Santiago between Espaillat and Av Mirador del Yaque. The city's largest agricultural market is a fascinating place to wander around. The roads leading in are lined with huge bins of beans, corn, bananas, tobacco, oregano, garlic and cassava, but these do little to capture the real atmosphere inside which has an almost timeless, mystic feel to it. Within the market, at the corner of 16 de Agosto and Espaillat, the local *botánica* sells portraits of *Santería* saints and potions whipped up on the spot for every conceivable malady, while in hidden back rooms it's possible to get your tarot cards read for a small fee.

Aurora Tabaclera

Jiménez 2 just off 27 de Febrero ☎241-1111. 9.30am–5pm, closed Sun. Free. At the authentic Aurora Tabaclera cigar factory, you can watch cigars being hand rolled, after which you're escorted to a lux smoking room to receive a free cigar, accompanied by Presidente on tap. On the whole, it's not as extensive a tour as you'll get at the Centro León Jimenes, but at least it's a real, working tobacco factory.

Estadio Cibao

Av Imbert and Domingo Bermúdez
℡575-1810. Tickets RD$100–200.
The winter-league baseball
games at Estadio Cibao, home
to Santiago's professional
baseball team, provide an
excitement unlike any other
attraction in town. The rowdy,
super-participatory crowd is
at least half the fun. Winter
games last from mid-November
through early February; book a
ticket in advance as the bigger
games can sell out.

Jacagua

10km northwest of town; accessible
only by car. Follow Estrella Sadhalá
west until you reach the "Plazanutty"
sign at the Carretera Jacagua, and
then go north. A left turn at the fork in
the road leads 2km to Jacagua. The
ruins of Jacagua – sixteenth-
century Santiago – are well
worth a visit, particularly if
you don't have time to check
out the more extensive ones
at La Vega Vieja. Conceived
as a gold-mining outpost, old
Santiago soon transformed into
an agricultural hub before being
swallowed in a catastrophic
earthquake in the late sixteenth
century, after which the city was
moved to its present location.
The stone foundations and
crumbling walls, many of them
pockmarked by weeds, are
scattered about the large private
plantation. You're free to wander
about, though it's difficult to
get any real sense of the town's
layout from what's left.

La Cumbre

9km north of Santiago. The
Carretera Turística treads
through lush, rolling mountains,
making for an incredibly scenic
drive to La Cumbre, home to
the largest system of amber
mines in the world, a setting

▲ VEGETABLES AT THE MERCADO HOSPIDAYE

(and inspiration) for the movie
Jurassic Park. Several roadside
souvenir stalls mark its location;
to reach the actual mines
take the turnoff marked "La
Cumbre de Juan Vegas" and
continue west 3km. From there
you'll have to hike a couple of
kilometres, up and over the top
of a hill, to the mine entrance.
The mines are extremely
basic, just deep holes in the
ground supported by gerry-
rigged wooden frames, with an
extensive network of tunnels
leading under the mountain
from the bottom of the pit. The
miners sell you chunks of amber
and may even be willing to lead
you down into one of the pits,
armed only with a flashlight and
a pick.

San José de las Matas

35km west of Santiago. A sleepy
hill station overlooking the
palm trees and plantations of the
northern Cordillera Central, San
José is most interesting during
the fiesta patronal – held in the
first week of August – when
hundreds of relatives return
from the States for the festivities,
and during Christmas, when
there's a horseback, candlelit
procession at night.

There's little to do within
town but take a leisurely walk
and admire the views; for one
such lookout, take the dirt

path behind the post office, on 30 de Marzo, to a cliff-top park with a good vantage over the neighbouring mountains. Most points of interest lie a bit outside San José, including Balneario Vidal Pichardo, a swimming hole 10km north at the confluence of Río Amina and Río Bao. Just as lovely is the Balneario Los Montones Arriba, an elevated mountain campo with the most spectacular views in the area; head 5km east on the road to Santiago, then 7km south to Los Montones. An even better balneario – La Toma del Río Antonsape – lies 8km further south at Mata Grande, a starting point for an arduous trek to Pico Duarte; to get there, continue 4km south from Los Montones and take a right at the fork in the road.

Accommodation

Aloha Sol

Calle del Sol 50 ☎583-0090, ⓕ583-0950, ⓦwww.alohasol.com. Modern hotel with a/c, TV and great hot showers, although the rooms are quite small. Right in the centre of the shopping district and a good alternative for those who want comfortable, Western-style

accommodation but can't afford the *Gran Almirante*. US$60–70.

Camp David

Carretera Turística Km 12 ☎276-6400 or 626-0587, ⓕ736-7165. A one-time Trujillo mountain home turned hotel and restaurant that's popular with wealthy Dominicans and a top choice for those who want to stay out of the city centre. Many of the large, comfortable rooms have balconies with stunning views over the city. Some of the toilets don't work properly, so inspect the bathroom before you accept a room. A museum on site houses many of the former dictator's cars including the one in which he was assassinated. US$50–70.

Centro Plaza

Mella 54 ☎581-7000, ⓕ582-4566, ⓔhcentroplaza@verizon.net.do. Spacious Western-style hotel, in an ideal central location, with huge, comfortable rooms and all the amenities you could wish for including a gym, an excellent restaurant and a stunning honeymoon suite with a 360-degree sweep of the entire city. Regular special offers make it even more attractive. US$60 for rooms, US$100 for honeymoon suite.

Colonial

Cucurullo and 30 de Marzo ☎247-3122, ⓕ582-0811. By far the best of the budget hotels, this well-kept, family-run place offers friendly service, clean rooms, a/c and TV. There are two separate buildings: one with rooms starting at US$15 but no a/c and only lukewarm water, the other for $10 more, with strong water pressure and a/c. US$15–30.

▲ TRUJILLO'S CARS IN THE CAMP DAVID MUSEUM

Don José

Colón 42 ☎581-7480. Large building with a small restaurant and clean budget-priced rooms in a useful central location. Rooms with private bathrooms and a/c are a bit more. US$7–12.

Gran Almirante

Estrella Sadhalá and Calle 10 ☎580-1992, ⓕ241-1492, ⓦwww.hodelpa .com. Elegant luxury hotel in a wealthy northeastern suburb with terrific service, tennis courts, swimming pool, three restaurants, a casino and a happening disco. If you've got the money, this is the place. US$100–155.

Hotel Restaurant San José

San José de las Matas, Calle 30 de Marzo 37 ☎578-8566. Comfortable budget hotel, with basic rooms, ceiling fans, hot water and friendly family proprietors who speak some English. Nothing to write home about, but a good place for a peaceful night's sleep. US$15.

Matún

Las Carreras 1 ☎583-5002, ⓕ581-8415. Recently renovated Trujillo-era hotel, perfect for those who want to enjoy Santiago's nightlife, as it's located right by the monument. Other advantages include a/c, cable TV and a casino. A good compromise if you want modern amenities but can't pay top dollar. US$45–55.

Restaurants

Camp David

Carretera Turística Km 12; look for turnoff and drive up winding road for 2km ☎223-0666. Former Trujillo mountain home, now converted into a gourmet restaurant and

▲ DAIQUI LOCO

hostelry (see opposite), that offers a long list of choice seafood dishes and steaks.

Cristobal

Gran Almirante Hotel, Estrella Sadhalá and Calle 10. Pricey, highly formal Castilian restaurant with delicious grilled red snapper, octopus, paella and garlic conch snail. The classy decor and quiet ambience make this an excellent spot for a date.

Daiqui Loco

JP Duarte and Oueste. Festive outdoor bar with the best grilled sandwiches and burritos in town, some for as little as RD$10. Frozen daiquiris are also a speciality. Definitely the place to watch the world go by.

El Encuentro

Argentina and Las Carreras. Popular outdoor hang-out near the monument that serves up tacos and other Mexican fast food. Big with working-class, college-age kids.

Montezuma

Av Francia in front of the monument. Best Mexican food in town in a relatively plush setting. The fajitas here are great but you're best off splurging on a heaping plate of grilled *camarones* smothered in garlic. They also have Corona and Dos Equis, which are hard to find elsewhere.

Olé

JP Duarte and Independencia. Creole restaurant serving Dominican staples and American-style pizzas in a thatch-sheltered terrace just off a small park – one of the prettiest dining areas in the entire city and conveniently close to most of the city's tourist attractions. Also has a take-out window.

Pancho

Restauración and JP Duarte. Neon-lit, Dominican fast-food joint with good fried chicken, RD$20 coffees and great breakfasts. Notable mainly as a good place to experience local culture, as it's wildly popular with city inhabitants and is a top-notch version of the *pica pollo* restaurants that dot the entire country.

Pez Dorado

Calle del Sol at Parque Altagracia. The granddaddy of elite Santiago dining, this institution has been around since the 1950s. High-end *comida criolla* in a fairly formal environment, including such tasty dishes as chicken with garlic, cilantro and olives, octopus, garlic shrimp, sea bass and also excellent Chinese offerings.

Puerto del Sol

Calle del Sol at the monument. *Comida criolla*, fast food and very cold beer served on a crowded open-air patio

▼ SANTIAGO NIGHTLIFE

with a memorable shot of the monument and great people-watching – though no Presidente beer because it's owned by a rival beer distributor.

Rancho Luna

Carretera Turística Km 7 ☎736-7176. Top-quality steakhouse and piano bar on the hill below Camp David, with excellent service, a huge wine list and great views over the city.

Las Tapas

Gran Almirante Hotel, Estrella Sadhalá and Calle 10. A casual tapas bar in the hotel courtyard, with a variety of good Spanish seafood appetizers, including pickled octopus, garlic shrimp and salted cod.

Bars

Bar Code

Cuba 22. Popular, laid-back courtyard bar with live Caribbean music and Latin jazz – definitely one of *the* places to hang out.

Biú

Estrella Sadhalá and Francia, behind the Hollywood 7 cinema complex. Hip new bar with a small dancefloor that draws large crowds early in the evening on weekends. Also has occasional live music or open bars (unlimited free drinks once you pay the cover charge).

Daiqui Loco

JP Duarte and Oueste. Outdoor, roadside bar with festive, relaxed atmosphere, the best daiquiris in town and a drive-through liquor window. You should definitely stop off here at least once.

Francifol
Calle del Sol 127 at Parque Duarte.
A classy, modern-looking pub
in a busy downtown area,
with some of the coldest beer
around. An excellent place for
drinks and conversation.

Karkoma
Monción 41. Left-leaning
hang-out decorated with
portraits of Latin American
revolutionaries and idealists,
Carnival photographs and
random memorabilia from the
early twentieth century. The
regulars here are basically the
Santiago intelligentsia, making
it a prime spot for interesting
conversation.

Kukaramacara
Av Francia in front of the monument.
The most happening spot in
the monument area, an open-
air building that's perpetually
packed with locals and features
late-night drum jam sessions,
great Dominican and Mexican
food, plus the obligatory cold
Presidentes and frozen tropical
drinks.

Pops
Av del Llano 1, behind the
Supermercado Nacional at Estrella
Sadhalá and 27 de Febrero. Popular
bar with good mixed drinks, a
large aquarium and a DJ spinning
a mix of merengue and rock. It
has remained one of the town's
hot spots for over ten years.

Talanca
Restauración and Tolentino.
Downtown reggae and jazz bar
with a great LP collection, plus
a courtyard that's shaded by a huge
oak tree. Boasts the most convivial
atmosphere in town, though the
crowds here are a little older than
at most of the college-student-
oriented bars and clubs.

▲ FRANCIFOL

Clubs and entertainment

Alcázar
Gran Almirante Hotel, Estrella Sadhalá
and Calle 10. Cover RD$100. The
best disco in town for travellers,
dominated by locals but very
safe and unintimidating. Features
a variety of music, but favours
the Latino sound; it doesn't get
hopping until 1am, and stays full
until 7am. Dress sharply.

Ambis I
Autopista Duarte Km 2. Cover
RD$50–RD$250 (for major live acts).
Jam-packed dance venue with
slick, American-style decor and
regular live music.

Dalí Café
JP Duarte 1. Lively joint with
mixed music, plenty of live
entertainment and karaoke.
Open-bar nights every Thursday
and some Sundays, with a cover
of RD$100 (men) and RD$50
(women).

Tribeca Lounge
Mauricio Alvarez 8. Hip new
nightclub geared toward a
wealthy young college crowd,
with the slick, dark feel of the
New York City neighbourhood
for which it was named. Also
a major hang-out for the local
rave scene.

The Cordillera Central

It's hard to believe you're in the Caribbean when exploring the Cordillera Central, a mighty mountain range blanketed by vast alpine forests that slices through the heart of the DR. Three national parks – all growing centres of eco-tourism – offer guided treks, white-water rafting, and waterfall rappelling. Mountain resorts, such as Jarabacoa, support visitors with a fine array of hotels, restaurants and adventure-tour outfits. A remote alternative base is Constanza, nestled between the highest peaks of the range. Wherever you go, remember that these are big mountains and should be explored with caution and proper gear – sturdy hiking boots, winter clothing and a waterproof coat. At the foot of the range sits the industrial town of La Vega, boasting the country's liveliest Carnival.

La Vega

30km southeast of Santiago. La Vega started out as one of Columbus's gold-mining towns, only to be levelled in a sixteenth-century earthquake and rebuilt as a farming community. Aside from the ruins of this old settlement, known as La Vega Vieja – well outside town – there's little in today's noisy, concrete city to hold your attention. However, La Vega's **Carnival** celebrations are generally acknowledged to be among the most boisterous and authentic in the nation. A twenty-block promenade is set up between the two main parks, along which parade platoons of demons in impressively horrific masks, the making of which is somewhat of a local speciality. Many city-dwellers who spend their days as hotel clerks, bankers or auto mechanics use much of their free time perfecting mask making; in addition to papier-mâché, they often incorporate materials like bull horns, bone and sharpened dogs' teeth. If you'd like to purchase a mask, try *Robert's Restaurant and Car Wash*, on the Carretera La Vega; expect to pay at least RD$700, depending upon how elaborate the design is.

Getting there and getting around

For the most part, the mountain roads in the Cordillera Central are truly horrific, and getting from one town to the next often requires a convoluted route; the easiest way to travel between Jarabacoa and Constanza, for example, is to leave the mountains via one paved road and then re-enter via another. The best access point to all major mountain sites is the Autopista Duarte that stretches between Santiago and Santo Domingo. To head deeper into the range you'll need a donkey; blazed trails lead to Pico Duarte from five separate points, with stops in secluded alpine valleys Tétero and Bao.

Santo Cerro

5km north of La Vega on Autopista Duarte; look for signed turnoff. Holy Hill marks the site of an important battle, sparked when Columbus led an inland expedition in 1494 to round up Tainos to give to his men as slaves. A large company of natives from the valley below attacked his troops, and supposedly the fight was not going well for the Spaniards until Columbus raised a large, wooden cross on the hill, an apparition of the Virgin perched atop it, and the emboldened Europeans slaughtered the enemy. It couldn't be more peaceful today, crowned by a beautiful brick church and an unbelievable view of the valley below. Within the sanctuary is an imprint purportedly marking where Columbus planted the cross.

La Vega Vieja

100m north of Santo Cerro; take turnoff west down a steep hill lined with crumbling religious statuary. Make a left at the end of the road to reach La Vega Vieja. Mon–Sat 9am–noon & 2–5pm. RD$30. These are the ruins of Columbus's original city, founded in 1494 after the Santo Cerro battle. The foundations on display, including a fortress, church, portions of the aqueduct and a few stone houses, make up only a tenth of the original city. The fort remains the most extensive ruin, with several of its walls intact; colonists plundered much of the stone in the nineteenth century to build the church at Santo Cerro. Just east of the main ruins, a partially intact Franciscan monastery sits peacefully on a hillside, with most of its outer walls still standing.

Jarabacoa

30km west of La Vega. A mountain resort peppered with coffee plantations, Jarabacoa draws wealthy Dominicans for its cool summers and lovely scenery. The pine-dominated mountains – dubbed rather inanely "The Dominican Alps" – immediately surrounding the town hold four large waterfalls, several rugged trails fit for day-hikes, three rivers used for white-water rafting and the busiest starting-point for treks of Pico Duarte. Due to a glut of construction, Jarabacoa's not as mellow as it once was, and you're best off residing away from the concrete town centre.

Downtown's small grid runs alongside the Río Yaque del Norte, with most of the action centred on a major crossroads

▲ COFFEE PLANTS NEAR JARABACOA

a few blocks north of the small Parque Central. The park is a great place to hang out on weekend evenings, when a couple hundred people mill about listening to music blare from trucks and drinking at a half-dozen storefront beer halls.

At the junction of Río Yaque del Norte and Río Jimenoa lies a popular weekend swimming spot, Balneario La Confluencia, with a small bar and a densely wooded park.

Lower Jimenoa Waterfall

3km east of Jarabacoa off the Carretera Jarabacoa, then accessible on foot via a rocky suspension bridge. Daily 8.30am–7pm. RD$10. The crashing Lower Salto Jimenoa is the most popular of Jarabacoa's waterfalls, boasting a deep pool good for swimming and staffed by a lifeguard. It's fun – if a bit nerve-wracking – to see the local kids jumping off high rocks into the water far below.

Baiguate Waterfall

1km south of Jarabacoa on the Constanza highway. Daily 8.30am–7pm. Free. The sixty-metre-high Salto Baiguate is a bit taller than the Lower Jimenoa, and instead of navigating the Jarabacoa town centre to get to its entrance, you'll have a pleasant half-kilometre hike through small farms and rural woods. There's a large swimming hole at the waterfall's base, plus a decent-sized cave where you can clamber around just behind the rush of water.

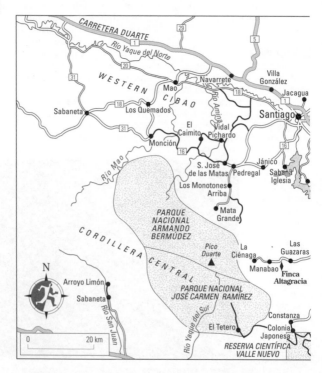

Jimenoa Uno Waterfall

7km south of Jarabacoa on the Constanza highway. Pass through a small pueblo before coming to a few shacks on the right; look for a small sign to the left. The steepest Jarabacoa-area waterfall by far is the Higher Salto Jimenoa, or Salto Jimenoa Uno, as it's often called. It isn't that easy to find but once you follow the steep footpath to the bottom and scramble over some huge slabs to the pool at the waterfall's base, you're rewarded with one of the island's most majestic spectacles. The cascading water drops 75m from a hidden lake above and thunders into a huge pool at its base, while the spray creates rainbow patterns on the rocky walls – it's easy to see why this was chosen for a scene in *Jurassic Park*. It's certainly worth the effort of getting here and you'll probably have the place to yourself.

▲ JIMENOA UNO WATERFALL

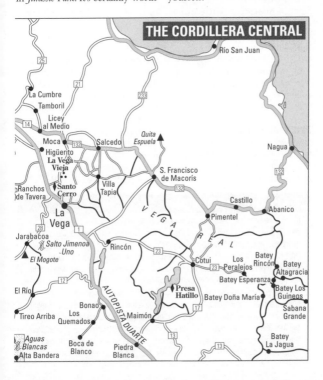

THE CORDILLERA CENTRAL

▲ GUIDED TRIPS UP PICO DUARTE

El Mogote hike

Two kilometres west of Jarabacoa you'll see a marked turnoff for El Mogote – best of the local day-hikes – a tall mountain with a trail that can be done in five hours round-trip; make sure to bring food and plenty of water, as the last stretch is extremely steep. At its base sits **Centro Salesiano**, a Salesian monastery where many of the Spanish monks have taken a vow of silence (though the administrator is happy to talk to visitors) which supports itself by running a pasta factory. There's also a Cistercian monastery a few metres up the trail.

Finca Altagracia

20km west of Jarabacoa; turn left off the Jarabacoa/Manabao road at the El Manguito sign and veer left at the cross in the road

ⓦwww.cafealtagracia. com. This huge organic coffee plantation, founded by author Julia Alvarez and her husband Bill Eichner, lies amid beautiful mountain landscapes and is home to large flocks of Hispaniolan parrots. Unlike many of the multinational operators, the farm welcomes visitors and can show you how coffee is grown and harvested. They'll also point you toward the best hiking trails and swimming holes in the area, and they offer reasonably priced accommodation (see p.149).

Pico Duarte

Park entrance fee RD$100. Two national parks, **Bermúdez** and **Ramírez**, each encompassing over seven hundred square kilometres, protect much of the mountains, cloudforests and pines in the Cordillera Central. The parks are best explored on an organized trek up Pico Duarte, the tallest mountain in the Caribbean. Two different strenuous treks lead up the 3087-metre Pico Duarte, which towers over the centre of the mountain range alongside its sister peak La Pelona ("Baldy";

Pico Duarte practicalities

If you intend to hike Pico Duarte, make sure to register and hire a guide at the park entrance no matter which of the trails you choose. One guide is assigned to every five people (RD$300/day plus meals); it's also a good idea to rent a mule (RD$400/day). You'll need to purchase enough food for yourself and the guide, plus an extra day and a half in case of emergency. Stock up on water as well, and bring purification tablets for any river water you might drink.

There are several very basic cabins with wood-burning stoves in which to sleep along the routes, but a couple of the treks will require tent camping for one night. Treks can be made any time of year, but most choose to ascend between November and March, when there's less chance of heavy rain. Regardless, never attempt the hike without a long waterproof coat with a hood, winter clothing (at night the temperature can reach freezing), a sleeping bag and good hiking boots.

before 1930 they were known as Pelona Grande and Pelona Chica). The lack of fresh water on the mountain has left it uninhabited through the centuries – though Tainos once lived in the nearby Tétero Valley – and it was ascended for the first time only in 1944. Today, though, it's done as a matter of course.

Climbing to the very top of the Caribbean's highest mountain holds definite cachet, and the view from the treeless peak is magnificent (though even here you can't quite escape from it all – Duarte's face is sculpted onto one of the rocks). If you've come this far, think seriously about extending your trek to include the **Tétero Valley** – a broad savannah with roaring mountain rivers, wild horses and Taino petroglyphs. This can be done by adding a two-day loop onto the La Ciénaga trek (see below) or by following one of the trails that crosses the valley on the approach to the peak. Unless you're a seasoned trekker, you'll do well to stick to the La Ciénaga route; you might also consider two **tour operators** who run trips up this trail: Iguana Mama (US$350; see p.167) and Rancho Baiguate (see p.173), with cheaper tours but fewer amenities.

La Ciénaga trail

25km west of Jarabacoa.
The most popular trip up Pico Duarte starts from the tiny pueblo of La Ciénaga, where you'll need to register for the 46-kilometre round-trip at the office by the park's entrance on the far side of the village. The best bet is to arrive in the afternoon, sort out the formalities and then camp down in the village with a view to starting out early the next morning. The first leg is little more than a comfortable four-kilometre riverside stroll to a bridge across the river at Los Tablones. Once over the river, however, the climbing starts for real and you'll gain over 2000m in the next 14km, mostly on a badly eroded track that winds its way through some wonderfully wild woodland. Regular stops at official picnic sites allow you to get your breath back and to peep out through the canopy for a glimpse of the totally pristine wilderness that surrounds you. You'll spend the night in a ramshackle cabin at La Compartición and then scramble up the last 5km at around 4.30am to be on the bare rocky summit for sunrise. It's quite a stirring sight to watch the sun creep over the horizon, casting a bright red hue

▲ HORSEBACK RIDING IN THE CORDILLERA CENTRAL

on the banks of cloud beneath your feet. You'll then backtrack to collect your belongings at the cabin and start the long descent back to the village.

Bonao

36km south of La Vega. Bonao's economy is supported single-handedly by the nearby Falconbridge ferronickel mine, an imposing industrial complex a kilometre south of town. With its enormous smokestacks, high-tech machinery, omnipresent security staff and fascist-looking falcon's-head logo emblazoned on everything from the front gate to the shuttle buses, the place resembles a caricature of evil straight out of a James Bond film. Like most mining towns, the city itself is pretty depressing – bleak, concrete and crowded with thousands of zigzagging, dustcloud-raising motorcycles – and holds nothing of particular interest, aside from a few pretty mock-gingerbread houses in Barrio Gringo at its northern end. Now that the Carnival at La Vega has become so touristy, though, an increasing number of people come here in February for a more authentic, equally wild celebration, attended mostly by locals.

Boca de Blanco

14km west of Bonao. For an idyllic detour, head for the piñon-covered mountains surrounding Bonao, best experienced by taking a scenic road southwest to the Boca de Blanco reservoir and dam. Turn east at Los Quemados – which has a couple of places to stop for lunch – and you'll find yourself amid some terrific mountain scenery, including views of two separate waterfalls. The reservoir itself, 15km further on the main road, is a perfect place for an afternoon picnic and a swim, and you're allowed to walk atop the dam.

Constanza

38km west of Bonao. Constanza is a drop-dead gorgeous, circular valley set deep in the mountains at an altitude of 1300m. Populated and farmed since the Taino era, it was created millennia ago by a meteor; as you first pass over the lip of the crater you'll be stunned by the fertile, flat valley – irrigated by thousands of sprinklers and hemmed in on all sides by jagged peaks. Constanza had virtually no contact with the outside world until the end of the nineteenth century, when a decent dirt road was finally blazed to it; later development occurred when Trujillo trucked in two hundred Japanese families in the 1950s, to introduce their farming methods to the valley. The town,

▲ CONSTANZA FIELDS

▲ CORDILLERA CENTRAL HIKING TRAIL

which takes up the western quarter of the valley, is mostly residential and fairly compact – as such you can make a quick go-round of it. The hub of activity is the **farmer's market** just north of Calle Luperón – the main thoroughfare – where truckloads of goods are loaded up and shipped to Santo Domingo. At the south end of town sits the decaying **Nueva Suiza**, an abandoned Trujillo manor that was used for a time as a resort spa but is now fenced off and boarded up, alongside a large greenhouse where you can buy orchids, hyacinths, roses and other flowers. (Roses can also be purchased from roadside shacks along the Carretera Constanza

for RD$30 apiece.) If you stay the night in Constanza, head to the eastern lip of the valley crater via the highway and check out the unbelievable sunset.

Aguas Blancas

10km south of Constanza on a ragged dirt road. The Constanza area's major sight is this torrential, 150-metre waterfall in three sections with a large pool at the base. The scenery alone is worth the somewhat difficult trek out – towering 2000-metre mountains veined with cavernous valley ribbons, half of it virgin pine forest and half terraced agriculture. Farms teeter on mountaintops so

Hiking in Constanza

The Constanza Valley boasts some of the DR's finest hiking trails. One three-hour trip sets off from the *Cabañas de las Montañas* hotel in Colonia Kennedy, which is just east of the main town. From the hotel, take the dirt road north until you reach a white house at the top of the hill, starting point of a trail that leads into the thick of the alpine forest. You can also set off 5km east of Constanza via the Carretera Constanza to the adjoining valley of **Tireo Arriba**, which holds a smaller farming pueblo worth exploring for a look at the local way of life. If you have your own transport, keep going 8km further east to pueblo **Las Palmas** – just before you reach the road to Jarabacoa – for a hike along the **Río Arroyazo**. Ask locals to direct you to the riverside walking path, from where it's a 45-minute hike to an unspoiled wilderness balneario, with small cascades along the river giving way to a large pool partially enclosed by boulders.

inaccessible you'll wonder how the building materials ever got there; look also for the many cattle that graze precariously along zigzagging paths worn into the steep mountainside.

Valle Nuevo

10km south of Constanza. The gutted, sky-high road that leads south from Constanza to San José de Ocóa offers an adventure, however hazardous, that you're not likely to forget. Do not attempt this unless you have an excellent 4WD and are a very experienced mountain driver – some sections have been so washed away that you'll have a difficult time navigating the road at all. Allow five hours and be sure to bring two spare tyres, winter clothing and emergency supplies.

The road runs through a national forest preserve known as **Reserva Científica Valle Nuevo**, a steep alpine wilderness with views that extend across much of the Cordillera Central, and for most of the trip you'll be skirting the edge of a cliff far above the clouds. You'll have to make a stop (and probably pay an RD$50 bribe) at the turnoff for the small military fort at **Alta Bandera**, 30km south of Constanza, where you can get a glimpse of a concrete pyramid built by Trujillo to mark the exact centre of the island.

Accommodation

Altocerro

Colonia Kennedy, Constanza ☎530-6192 or 6181, ☏530-6193, ✉cmatis@verizon.net.do. Reasonably priced small hotel with comfortable rooms. Also available are some private villas and camping facilities for those

looking for an up-close-to-nature experience. They have a decent restaurant and offer horseback excursions, bike rental and weekend outdoor barbecues for guests. US$25–35.

Anacaona

La Confluencia, Jarabacoa ☎574-2686. Modern, tastefully decorated self-catering apartments with a useful full kitchen and hot-water showers. Close to the baseball field, a little outside of town – all the better for a peaceful night's sleep. US$30–50.

Aquarius

Duarte 104, Bonao ☎296-2898, ☏296-2360, ☒www.aquariusbonao. com. If you're stuck in Bonao for the night, this brand new hotel, disco and shopping complex that's decked out to look like a big turquoise aquarium is the only place for high quality and comfort. Standard rooms come with high-speed Internet access; top-floor suites are available; and there's a swimming pool to boot. US$50 for rooms, $75 for suites.

Brisas del Yaque

Luperón, Jarabacoa ☎574-4490. Clean, modern hotel near the town centre. The rooms are quite small but come with a/c, TV and fridge. Best place to stay if you want to be in the action, but sometimes gets noisy. US$25.

Cabañas de las Montañas

Colonia Kennedy, Constanza ☎539-3268. Spacious modern villas with full kitchens and all the amenities, set on the lip of the valley and surrounded by thousands of wildflowers. The staff organize tours, including half-day hikes into the mountains behind the hotel and a trip to the nearby cascades at La Parma. US$40.

Finca Altagracia

La Ciénaga road Km 17, Los Dajaos ⒲www.cafealtagracia.com. Set within some of the most beautiful mountain country you'll ever see, this working organic coffee farm offers accommodation with three meals included. Come here for the isolation and an intimate look at campesino life. You can choose between dorm beds with latrine and shared shower, a large "matrimonio" suite with private cold-water bath and bare mattresses, and a couple of relatively nice guest rooms with private hot-water bath and bedding. The excellent food, mostly vegetarian and organic, comes straight from the farm, and includes typical country Dominican cuisine like *sancocho*, rice and beans, yucca fritters and *tostones*. US$15–35.

Gran Jimenoa

Av La Confluencia, Los Corralitos, 2km east of centre of Jarabacoa ⒯574-6304, ⒡574-4345, ⒠hotel puntojimenoa@verizon.net.do. A new riverside hotel in a three-storey building. Large rooms come with a/c and TV, and overlook a pleasant pool and hot tub. Some rooms offer excellent river views. US$65, includes breakfast.

Hogar

Mella 34, Jarabacoa ⒯574-2739. The best budget hotel in Jarabacoa, with private showers, clean rooms and a pleasant courtyard. That said, you shouldn't expect luxury. You can also hire a motoconcho guide here to take you on a tour of the waterfalls and balnearios (RD$300). US$14.

Jarabacoa River Resort

La Confluencia, Jarabacoa ⒯574-4688. Modern private cabañas with hot water, kitchen, three bedrooms, two baths and swimming pool. Extremely comfortable but self-catering and probably better suited to groups or families. US$65.

Pinar Dorado

Constanza highway Km 1, Jarabacoa ⒯574-2820, ⒡574-2237, ⒠pinardorado@verizon.net.do. Pleasant hotel, owned by the *Baiguate* group, with TV, a/c, hot water, private balconies, restaurant and bar. More comfortable than *Rancho Baiguate* and an ideal base for some of the group's excursions. Recently renovated, it now offers a good-value meal option as well. US$35.

Rancho Baiguate

Constanza highway Km 5, Jarabacoa ⒯574-6890, ⒡574-0000, ⒲www.ranchobaiguate.com. Sprawling ranch with basic rooms, plus a football pitch, basketball court, ping-pong table, swimming pool, horse ranch, fishing pond and organized adventure excursions. No hotel service at night, but a perfect place if you're looking for peace and quiet – and still want easy access to the town. Price includes three buffet meals. US$45.

Rancho Wendy

2km west of Bonao on the Boca de Blanco highway, just outside Los Quemados village ⒯630-1261, ⒲www.ranchowendy.com. Quiet, idyllic little spot with clean but no-frills rooms and dorm beds, and also a swimming pool and several horses for riding into the nearby hills. If you prefer to camp, you can pitch your tent on their sprawling property for

US$5. They also offer good, simple meals, though these are not included in the room price. US$10–25.

Restaurants

Don Luis
Colón and Duarte at Parque Central, Jarabacoa. Good mid-range restaurant facing the park, with steak, seafood and the usual Dominican staples. Great place to eat on weekends, when the Parque Central is packed with locals hanging out and having a good time.

Galería El Parque Pizzeria
Duarte at Parque Central, Jarabacoa. Inexpensive, fun outdoor pizza spot especially popular with families. The pies are excellent, though sometimes topped with odd "only in the Dominican Republic" combos like jalapeño peppers and corn.

Jalapeño
Duarte, one block south of Parque Central, Jarabacoa ⊛ www .jalapenojarabacoa.com. Authentic little Mexican restaurant, a rarity in this country, with delicious fajita platters for two as well as tacos and extremely cheesy quesadillos and nachos. Ask for the cold ginger tea to wash it all down.

JL Comedor
Parque Central just off the baseball field, Constanza. Best little comedor in town for sampling Dominican staples, with huge portions for less than RD$100 a plate.

Lorenzo's
Luperón 83, Constanza. The elevator music tends to grate here, but the food is terrific, including steak smothered in onions, guinea hen al vino and coco con leche for dessert.

El Mogote
Libertad and Piña, Jarabacoa. Unpretentious 1950s diner atmosphere with RD$30 greasy but tasty Dominican specials. They also serve the finest café con leche in town.

La Montaña
Ureña 40 at Parque Anacaona, Constanza. A pleasantly rustic atmosphere where you can enjoy treats like roasted guinea hen, or just a simple breakfast of croissants.

La Parrillada
Calle Independencia, Jarabacoa. A top-notch grill-house with excellent *criolla* dishes including guinea fowl in wine plus the usual goat and fish. Especially popular on weekends.

El Rancho
Main crossroads at town entrance, Jarabacoa. Another part of the *Baiguate* empire, this excellent high-end restaurant serves pizza plus specialities like baked chicken stuffed with banana, garlic soup, crepes, seafood and steaks. Nice ambience, too – the walls are littered with art by top Dominican painters.

Restaurant Típico Bonao
Autopista Duarte at Bonao town entrance. One of the most famous restaurants in the entire country, this indoor thatch-roofed spot is a required stop for locals travelling the Autopista Duarte between Santiago and Santo Domingo. Dig into high-end *criolla* cuisine, including excellent soups, lobster and garlic shrimp.

Clubs and entertainment

Antillas

Av Independencia at Jarabacoa's main crossroads. Best disco in Jarabacoa, set in a circular two-storey building with the rustic, wood-slat decor of most rural Dominican dance halls. They play popular merengue and bachata hits and it's a great place to meet locals.

Aquarius Bar

Duarte 104, Bonao ⓦ www .aquariusbonao.com. Cover RD$100 for men, RD$50 for women. Slick nightclub in the heart of Bonao with a nightly tag-team DJ combo that spins techno, drum 'n' bass and Latin rap. By far the hippest place in town, the kind of club you'd expect only in Santo Domingo. Thursday is Ladies Night and there's a Friday happy hour from 8–10pm.

Engini Car Wash

Cáceres and Restauración, La Vega. Second-floor bar/restaurant above the car wash with a small dancefloor. La Vega's liveliest hang-out, with relatively hip decor, a fun crowd, and pool tables.

Estadio Jarabacoa

La Confluencia, just west of town crossroads, Jarabacoa. You'd be mad to miss Jarabacoa's nightly baseball games. In addition to the spirited play on the field, there's a bar in the dugout and the outfield abuts an outdoor pool hall – all in all, a great way to spend an evening relaxing and getting to know some locals.

Neblinas Café

Duarte and Ureña, Constanza. Great little bar in downtown Constanza with a strong local following that nets most of the top live acts that come to town. A friendly crowd and two dozen international beers, a host of mixed drinks (try the local speciality, an Aguas Blancas), Perrier and so forth.

Plaza Central

Sánchez and Colón at Parque Central, Jarabacoa. The town's modern disco, always crowded late at night, and with a relatively sophisticated light and sound system.

▲ ANTILLAS DISCO

The Southwest

The rural Southwest curves along the Caribbean, its nominal centre the city of Barahona, an old sugar-processing capital that has seen better days. Inland, vast tracts of sugar cane take over the countryside. The main towns – from Barahona and Azua to Baní and San Cristóbal – have long been courting all-inclusive hotels to the area's many superb beaches, but environmentalists are lobbying hard to stop any development, particularly along Parque Nacional Jaragua's beachfront. For now, this means that the coastline is almost completely undeveloped, quite an attraction in itself for independent travellers who don't mind roughing it a bit. The top beaches lie at San Rafael and El Pato, where massive waterfalls snake down mountains and form large swimming holes that pour into the sea.

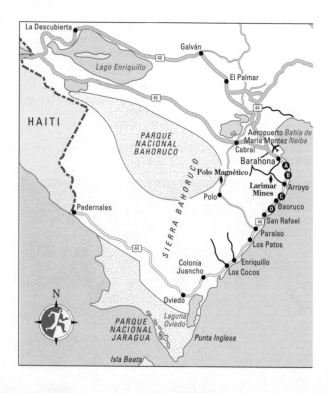

Getting there and getting around

Most visitors arrive via guagua or car; coastal Highway 44 (called the Carretera Sánchez) connects the city with Azua, Baní and Santo Domingo to the east before continuing west all the way to the border. Guaguas pick up and drop off at all major towns along the coast, and there are also regular routes that lead north to San José de Ocóa. The Carretera Sánchez is well paved and fairly easy to navigate by car, though west of Barahona you should watch out for some tricky turns atop high cliffs. Be prepared also for the highway to end abruptly at the major towns, only recommencing at the other side. Off the main highway you'll usually have to make do with rough dirt roads, though paved avenues lead from the Carretera to San José de Ocóa, Cabral, Las Salinas and Palenque.

San Cristóbal

22km west of Santo Domingo. There's little reason to spend time in Trujillo's hometown, which obviously enjoyed its heyday during his rule, and was the beneficiary of an enormous cathedral and two palatial presidential residences. The cathedral still stands – though there's little reason to visit it – but the mansions are now in ruins, and the cramped, asphalt city qualifies as one of the country's least appealing.

Casa Caoba

2km north of San Cristóbal. Daily 8am–5pm. Yet another abandoned Trujillo mansion, the stylish

THE SOUTHWEST

ACCOMMODATION
Bahoruco Beach Resort — C
Barahona Coral Sol — D
Casablanca — A
Club Hotel Quemaito — B

The Southwest PLACES

▲ THE SOUTHWEST COAST BY NIGHT

1938 Casa Caoba was originally built entirely out of mahogany and has clean, stylized angles reminiscent of Frank Lloyd Wright. The manicured Japanese gardens surrounding it are now going to weed, and though plans to convert the mansion into a historical attraction have been hyped for years, only modest renovation has been completed. You'll have to make do with the guard's informal tour, which navigates through the various rooms, including a secret chamber through which the dictator's mistress was conducted to his bedroom, and a look at the intricately crafted, stacked woodwork still waiting to be cleaned up.

La Toma

9km north of Casa Caoba. Daily 8.30am–7.30pm. RD$10 and parking RD$50 or RD$10 guagua from the San Cristóbal Parque Central.
Unbelievably popular with locals on weekends, La Toma consists of large cemented pools supplied with fresh water from the Río Haina. The water is surprisingly clean, but the best reason to visit is for a slice of local Dominican life, as hundreds of families hang out here, splashing around in the water and generally cutting loose.

Reserva Arqueológica El Pomier

11km north of San Cristóbal. Daily 9.30am–5pm. RD$50 park entrance, plus $350 for a guide; bring your own flashlight and wear boots. El Pomier protects the most extensive collection of cave pictographs in the Caribbean – some as many as 2000 years old – though this claim to notoriety draws few visitors. There are three major sets of caves, but El Pomier is the only one open to the public. Upon arrival, you'll be assigned a park guide (Spanish-speaking only) who'll take you to the first of three enormous, easily accessible chambers, two of which hold a variety of Taino pictographs. In addition to scattered depictions of various birds and animals (which were once used for religious rituals) there are a number of interesting geological formations and one cave filled with thousands of bats. If you want to see the best petroglyphs, though, you're in for a bit of an adventure, including rappelling down steep cave walls. Note that the El Pomier caves may be closed at some point for renovations.

Playa Najayo and Playa Palenque

14km south of San Cristóbal, along the Carretera Palenque; guaguas depart regularly from the San Cristóbal Parque Central. Playa Najayo has a terrific strip of beige sand and several decent restaurants. A bit more crowded, Palenque was named for a *cimarrón* encampment that survived here until the late eighteenth century. The beach at the town's western end has remarkably calm waters, perfect for lazing about, though you'll be joined by plenty of others, especially on weekends. A dozen or so bustling bar/restaurants line the beach entrance.

Baní

36km west of San Cristóbal. Coastal Baní has in recent years turned relatively prosperous, thanks to a nearby naval base and the saltpans south of the city, an upswing that has spurred much population growth, if not exactly prettified the place. There are few diversions within town – the Parque Central is nice enough for people watching, and you can stop off at Botánica Chango on Duvergé and Carretera Las Calderas for a look at the wares used in the local folk religion. There's also an interesting fiesta patronal held in mid-June in honour of San Juan Bautista, with dozens of musicians performing a distinctive Afro-Latin music called sarandunga, which has heavy rhythmic influences from Senegal but is unique to Baní. Just outside town you'll find a number of pleasant beaches, including the one most frequented by locals, **Playa Los Almendros**, 5km south of the Parque Central on Calle Duarte. It's not as spectacularly scenic as its competitors along the Barahona coast, but is serviceable enough.

Las Salinas

16km southwest of Baní at the end of Carretera Las Calderas and 2km east of Las Calderas

naval facility. One of the more beautiful villages along the Southwest Coast, rural, quiet Las Salinas has a dozen houses scattered about a beautiful white-sand beach, and is surrounded by dunes, saltpans and rolling hills. It's a great place for windsurfing and the small resort *Salinas High Wind Center* (see p.161) serves as an informal windsurfing club on weekends – though you'll have to bring your own equipment.

San José de Ocóa

27km north of Carretera Sánchez along Highway 41. Tucked away in the mountains along the Río Nizao, the easygoing hamlet of San José de Ocóa consists mostly of clapboard shacks and is unremarkable but for its majestic setting, perched atop a high hill with views stretching across the southern Cordillera Central. Most come to visit the local river balneario **El Manantiel**, which draws weekenders from across the country (though few foreign visitors), mainly in the summer months when temperatures in the valley below can be sweltering. You'll find several good spots for swimming among the boulders and ice-cold cascades. Plenty of others – particularly families – opt for the outfits that siphon off fresh water from the river into large swimming pools, such as **Las**

▲ SALTPANS NEAR LAS SALINAS

Jessicas (daily 8.30am–10pm; RD\$10), down a steep incline on the opposite side of the road, where there's a diving board and a water slide. It also turns into a popular dance hall at night.

Azua

49km west of Baní. Established in 1504 by the future conqueror of Cuba, Diego Velázquez, Azua is among the oldest cities in the New World. In the early sixteenth century, Mexico conquistador Hernán Cortes served as its mayor, but despite this lofty history, there's nothing left of the original city, which was demolished by a 1751 earthquake. It's not surprising then that visitors usually just pass right through, though there is one decent beach, five-kilometre-long **Playa Monte Río**, a few kilometres south of town, with beautiful views of the rolling El Número mountains. To reach the beach, take the turnoff at the Brugal sign on Azua's eastern edge. Fishing boats bob on its calm waters and a few

locally run outdoor restaurants serve grilled fresh fish with the requisite accompaniments of plantains, rice and beans. A half-kilometre west, **Playa Blanca** is even more attractive, a placid turquoise cove with pure-white sand – though unfortunately home to a large number of sand fleas at night.

Barahona

60km west of Azua. Haitian General Touissant L'Ouverture founded Barahona in 1802 as an alternate port to Santo Domingo and, for a time, Trujillo based his multimillion-dollar sugar industry here. Since then, the city has fallen on hard times due to the low price of sugar globally and the transition in the US from sugar to corn syrup in all manner of sweetened products. Evidence of this downturn abounds in the uncared-for roads rutted to the point of near-impassability. In truth, Barahona is of use mostly as a base camp: the hotels are more plentiful and a bit better than the few along the coast

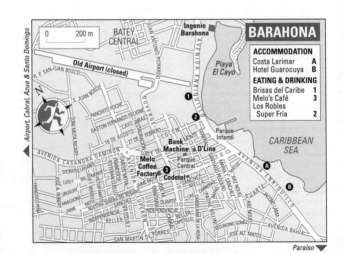

▲ BARAHONA MALECÓN

west of the city, and it's close enough to make easy day-trips to the beaches or even to Lago Enriquillo.

The **Malecón**, also known as Avenida Enriquillo, gets crowded with food shacks and partying locals at night; its major landmark is a **Parque Infantil** (children's park) on Calle Uruguay with a slide in the shape of the solar system. West from the park, past a series of beach shacks, lies a modest stretch of sand bordered by mangroves along the *Hotel Guarocuya*. The town's top public beach, though, unfolds at the opposite end of the boardwalk beyond **Ingenio Barahona**, the country's largest sugar mill, now saddled with debt and only sporadically functioning. From the mill, follow the mud track along the water for a half-kilometre to the peninsula at Barahona's far eastern end, which is ringed by pristine white sand and backed by palms.

Laguna Cabral

15km northwest of Barahona; guaguas depart hourly from the Barahona Malecón. The small town of Cabral sits on the eastern edge of the Parque Nacional Bahoruco, which protects the rugged, undeveloped mountain landscape covering the entire Southwest Coast, and is home to the serene **Laguna Cabral** (also known as Laguna Rincón). Numerous birds flock to this lovely lagoon, from Orilla, Criolla and Florida ducks to flamingos, ibises and herons. You can visit on a two-hour boat tour from the park station at the north end of town (RD$50 entrance fee, RD$800 for a boat plus RD$400 for a guide), or independently by heading north on the paved road that skirts the lagoon to the east to a pueblo called El Peñon, from where a dirt road leads west of town to the lagoon.

Lago Enriquillo

47km west of Barahona. Boat tours (2.5 hours; prices start at RD$100) depart daily at 7.30am, 8.30am and 1pm from the park entrance, near the lake's northwestern tip. Forty-two kilometres long and slightly larger than the island of Manhattan, this placid saltwater lake at the southern base of the Sierra Neiba mountain range sits at the lowest point in the Caribbean, a full 46m below sea level. If you're not content with circling the lake and seeing it from land, embark on one of the boat tours that explore an enormous bird sanctuary filled with flamingos and hundreds

▼ LAGO ENRIQUILLO

▲ IGUANA ON ISLA CABRITOS

of other tropical birds – an unforgettable multicoloured spectacle. Also a hit are the American crocodiles that inhabit this part of the lake, though you should take one of the morning tours if you want to see them – guides get in the water and steer the crocodiles past the boat for a closer view. Next stop on the tour is the arid, iguana-infested Isla Cabritos in the lake's centre, a sandy island covered with cactus where the half-tame rhinoceros iguanas crowd around you in the hopes of being fed.

Polo Magnético

10km south of Cabral on Carretera Polo. The Magnetic Pole is the stuff of rural legend, a place where the law of gravity is apparently defied. At an upward incline in the highway, marked by a roadside billboard, you can pull off on the right-hand fork and put your car in neutral; it will seem to be slowly pulled up the hill, as will any round object that you place on the pavement. A group of student surveyors from Santo Domingo's Catholic University established that the "pole" is an optical illusion,

but most locals believe that the miracle results from the presence of magnetically charged ore beneath the road's surface.

Playas Saladilla, Quemaito and Baoruco

West of Barahona along Highway 44. The entire coast west of Barahona is dotted with lovely beaches – with nary a soul on them. The placid sand cove Playa Saladilla offers shallow, calm waters great for swimming, while 3km further on is another equally sheltered spot, Playa Quemaito, with two small independent hotels on its shores. The largest area beach, and the most popular with Dominicans, lies 5km west of Quemaito in the tiny fishing village of Baoruco. The beach boasts exceptionally soft white sand and a couple of small resorts. Aside from the hotels, though, it's a sleepy place, where you can sprawl out on the sand and observe the goings-on of small-town Dominican life.

San Rafael, Paraíso and Los Patos

5–12 km beyond Baoruco. San Rafael has an enticing beach, though with a strong, crashing surf, that fills with Dominicans on weekends but remains only moderately populated the rest of the week. Fortunately for swimmers, a waterfall thrums down the nearby mountains and forms a natural pool at the entrance, with an unobtrusive manmade barrier walling it in so that water slowly pours over the edge into the sea. This area is a popular camping spot, complete with public shower and bathroom facilities, and some nearby shacks serving excellent grilled lobster and fresh fish. If you want to hike, climb up the mountains along the river's cascades for a few kilometres. Watch also for the turnoff just west of the beach, with panoramic views atop a high cape. Directly above the beach on a Sierra Bahoruco foothill is the **Villa Miriam**, a private complex (RD$200) with exclusive access to some of the best cascades, which it has cordoned off and turned into a popular local balneario. Paraíso, another 5km to the west, is the biggest town along this stretch, but doesn't offer much in the way of facilities. It does have a long strand of superb sandy beach, though there's precious little shelter from the beating sun. A much better beach lies yet 5km further west in Los Patos, where the ocean is joined again by a river descending from the mountains to form a freshwater swimming pool. The beach, surrounded by dense mangroves, stays quite active throughout the week, with plenty of beach vendors.

Los Blancos and Enriquillo

11km west of Los Patos. Tucked beneath a series of high, wide cliffs, the small pueblo of Los Blancos offers a quiet, pebbly beach that's usually devoid of visitors. Nearby Enriquillo, another 2km beyond Los Blancos, sits majestically over a jagged limestone precipice; a broad pebble beach stretches to the west, but there are no trees along it and thus little respite from the sun. Perched at the edge of a sheer cliff directly above the beach is the most scenic *club gallístico* in the country, with RD$20 cockfights on Saturdays.

Oviedo and Parque Nacional Jaragua

22km west of Enriquillo. Daily 9.30am–4pm. Park admission RD$50, payable at the national park office on the south side of Highway 44 just before the town and lagoon entrance. A small desert town with little in the way of facilities, Oviedo is worth a visit strictly as an entryway to Parque Nacional Jaragua, particularly the scenic **Laguna Oviedo** that lies at its entrance. The lake is often white with salt and gets minimal visitation, which enhances the starkly beautiful, seemingly extraterrestrial terrain. Dotting the lagoon are 24 islands, some with iguanas, which you can visit on lagoon tours. A boat captain in Oviedo does boat trips and you can also contact Grupo Jaragua (☎472-1036, ⒺJaragua@tricom.net) who have trained a number of local guides; ask at the small national park office at the lagoon entrance for one of the "voluntarios de jaragua", including a particularly good local guide named Pablito.

Accommodation

Bahoruco Beach Resort

Baoruco ☎524-1111, Ⓕ524-6060, Ⓔbarcelobahoruco@verizon.net.do. All-inclusive resort with 105 excellent rooms, a verdant pool area and private access to the southern end of Playa Baoruco. As usual, the buffet food is uninspiring – but at least it's included free with your room.

▼ LOCALS AT THE CASCADES

US$70–125, depending on the view.

Barahona Coral Sol

3km west of Baoruco on Highway 44 ☎ 524-4077, ⊛ www.coralsolresort .com. You'll have to look closely to find the entrance from the highway to this hidden gem, another of the independent resorts that have cropped up in and around Baoruco in the past few years. Perched rather precariously on a high cliff above the water, the grounds are beautiful and walking paths zigzag up and down the steep hillsides. The rooms have strong fans, balconies with ocean views, two bathrooms each, and are agreeably private, but keep in mind that as with most Dominican-centric resorts, service is nonexistent outside of mealtimes. Breakfast is included in the price. US$60.

Casablanca

Quemaito ☎ & ⊕ 471-1230, ⊜ susannaknapp@yahoo.de. The accommodation may be simple – rooms have private cold-water bath and fan – but the secluded natural beauty and gourmet cuisine more than make up for it. Cabañas are spread along rambling rural grounds on a clifftop overlooking a pebble beach. What draws people here is the food, which is truly outstanding (see opposite). US$25–35 with an additional US$10 for dinner.

Club Hotel El Quemaito

Quemaito ☎ 223-0999, ⊜ c.elquemaito@verizon.net.do. If you prefer a/c and hot water over haute cuisine, bypass the rustic cabins at *Casablanca* and instead head next door to this more modern hotel, a smallish resort with good facilities, a swimming pool and patio, and unremarkable but well-kept rooms with pretty ocean views. The vibe here is fairly relaxed – the favorite pastime is to hang out poolside and listen to moderate-volume merengue with a cooler of beer. US$25–40.

Costa Larimar

Malecón, Barahona ☎ 524-3442. The nicest accommodation in the entire region, with just about everything you could want from a Caribbean hotel – majestic views of the mountains and sea and meticulously clean rooms with a/c, television, telephone and even room service. The lovely grounds encompass a small stretch of mangroves and a private beach. That said, the price is absurdly high for this area and it remains to be seen whether they'll make a go of it in the long run. You're best off going non-all-inclusive, as the mediocre meals add about US$30 nightly. US$65–100.

Gran Marquiz

Baoruco ☎ 524-6866. An intimate little hotel on the Baoruco beach, with modest but clean hot-water rooms that sit right on the sand. A reasonable breakfast and dinner are included in the price. US$40.

Hotel Paraíso

Paraíso ☎ 243-1080. A decent budget hotel on the Paraíso waterfront. Though a lot less luxurious than nearby resorts, it's also a lot less expensive. Some rooms have a/c, some fan only; all come with cable TV, hot water and comfortable beds. US$12–20.

Sagrato de Jesús

Cañada and San José, San José de Ocoa ☎ 558-2432. No-frills

family-run pensión that's not especially luxurious but perfectly acceptable, with private warm-water showers, a/c and cable TV. It's the most comfortable place to stay in San José, and there's a good cafetería attached. US$16.

Salinas High Wind Center

Puerto Hermosa 7, Las Salinas ☎310-8141. A small resort catering mostly to wealthy Dominicans that has a pool, bar, disco and patio restaurant, and serves as an informal windsurfing club on weekends. The setting is beautiful – sand dunes everywhere, and placid Caribbean waters lapping a small private beach. Rooms are garishly painted but modern and comfortable, with good water pressure, a rarity in these parts. The attached disco gets noisy on weekends so try for a room in the annex across the street from the main building. The restaurant here (see p.162) is also one of the country's best, so it's well worth opting for the all-inclusive meal plan. The downside is that there's no service late at night and, if you need to make a phone call from the hotel, you'll have to buy a Verizon card in one of the town's *colmados*. They're also hard to reach by phone. US$60.

Restaurants

Baco

Parque Central, San José de Ocóa. Something of a town institution, this restaurant has been around for thirty years, probably because they do first-class renditions of classic Dominican home cooking. They're also quite cheap – a complete meal with roast chicken or *chivo*

guisado (goat stew) with rice, beans and plantains sets you back only about RD$100.

Brisas del Caribe

Malecón, Barahona ☎524-2794. A semi-formal seafood restaurant with sweeping views of the ocean, impeccable service and a slew of great menu offerings, including *camarones al ajillo, mero estilo bari*, lobster *a la plancha* and kingfish *al limón*. Pricey by Dominican standards but still a bargain at around US$25 per person. It's also the only place on the island where you're likely to be served a large Presidente bottle in a champagne ice-bucket.

Casablanca

El Quemaito. Even if you don't stay at the attached hotel, you can dine here (US$20 per person) provided you reserve two nights in advance. The proprietor is a gourmet French chef and serves dinner according to the *table d'hôte* tradition, by which customers tell her what they want for dinner in the morning, she goes to the market and buys everything fresh, prepares it, and everyone sits around a common table for the evening meal.

Gran Segovia

Azua. Surprisingly nice restaurant in the heart of this down-at-heels town, with a small formal dining room that specializes in local seafood, including shrimp plates (fried, creole or in garlic sauce), whole lobsters and grilled red snapper. The fresh food and reasonable prices make up for the somewhat stuffy atmosphere.

Mary Federal Restaurant

Pedernales. In Pedernales, half the people are fishers by trade, and here you can share in the local bounty – the freshest, most delicious fish in the entire country. This terrific restaurant, near the town beach, offers excellent grilled fish, lobster and *lambí* – and an especially spicey creole sauce – for around RD$120 a plate.

Melo's Café

Anacaona 12, Barahona ☎524-5437. Unpretentious diner with great home-cooking, including delicious American breakfasts (try the French toast) and fruit shakes, plus nightly dinner specials at 7pm for RD$85; don't miss the goat dish with banana, plantain and avocado.

Salinas High Wind Center

Las Salinas. Nowhere in the Dominican Republic can you dine on seafood in such an archetypally Caribbean setting. Stick to the *criolla* preparations of the lobster, dorado and *chillo*, as the creole sauce is truly out of this world. As you dine like a king, you'll stare out at a placid, glassy turquoise slice of sea, framed by rolling sand dunes and with a gazebo poking out into the water from the restaurant patio. Look to spend around US$15–20 per person for dinner.

San Rafael beach shacks

San Rafael. Quality seafood doesn't get cheaper than this. The shacks that line the waterfall and beach at the little pueblo of San Rafael serve up charcoal-grilled whole fish and lobster for less than RD$100, plus they're always stocked with plenty of ice-cold Presidente. All this and a view of both the ocean and a tumbling waterfall.

Clubs and entertainment

La Bella Juliana

San José de Ocóa. The biggest of several bars and dance halls along the highway at the town's main entrance, this is the place to discover campesino-style nightlife. It looks fairly modest but hosts some terrific merengue dancing and also has two pool tables.

Car Wash

Carretera Sánchez, 2km west of Azua. A traditional Dominican car wash/dance hall – the concrete area where they wash cars by day becomes a *típico* disco at night, drawing in a couple hundred locals every evening.

El Chapuzón

Just outside Baní, Carretera Salinas Km 2. This terrific outdoor spot vibrates with live music every weekend, including some of the country's top bachateros (from Raulín Rodríguez to Luis Vargas), making it one of the island's pre-eminent live-music venues. The decor is self-consciously campesino, with a thatch-roof central dancefloor.

Salinas High Wind Center

Las Salinas. The wealthy kids from the capital come here to dance, which means the music is more eclectic than anywhere else in this region, and includes American alternative rock, Latin rock and rap, hip-hop and electronica. On weekends the party extends into the wee hours.

Arrival

There are international **airports** on the south coast at Santo Domingo, the north coast at Puerto Plata, the east coast at Punta Cana and the central region at Santiago. Punta Cana is given over entirely to charter flights from North America and Europe, Santiago is used almost exclusively by Dominican expats, and the other two airports see a good mix of both. The majority of holidaymakers get their charter flight and free ground transport to their hotels in the price of their all-inclusive package;

if you're travelling independently you'll have to make do with the taxi flotillas that beseige each airport or rent a car. Each relevant chapter has a "Getting there" box that details airport locations and onward transport.

There's also a **ferry** service from Mayagüez, Puerto Rico, into Santo Domingo; the other way to arrive by water is as part of a cruise **ship** itinerary – unless you have your own boat.

Information

The glossy promotional materials handed out by Dominican consuls and tourist agencies are pretty to look at but seriously lacking in hard facts. The Dominican government also maintains **tourist offices** and **toll-free tourist hotlines** in the UK (☎0800/899-805), Canada (☎1-800/563-1611) and the US (☎1-888/358-9594), which are good for hooking you up with tour operators and package travel agents. The car rental agencies provide a basic **road map** that can get you to the major towns, but Rough Guides puts out a far more detailed map (available from ☎www.roughguides.com) to help find your way around. Mountain trekkers should look for the outstanding topographical map of the Cordillera Central in *Caminatas al Pico Duarte*, a booklet published by the Dominican National Parks Department in Santo Domingo (☎472-4204).

Useful websites

☮ **www.activecabarete.com** Comprehensive Cabarete site that lists all hotels, restaurants, watersports operators and other businesses in town.
☮ **www.debbiesdominicantravel.com** A dizzying array of links to hundreds of Dominican-related sites and a deep archive of travellers' accounts of all-inclusive vacations at every resort on the island.
☮ **www.dr1.com** The most heavily trafficked Dominican message board, and one of the best places to get Dominican Republic info on the Web.
☮ **www.hispaniola.com** A site dedicated to Dominican tourism, with a Dominican Spanish phrasebook, daily weather, a message board and an interactive Cabarete map.
☮ **www.iguanamama.com** Detailed info

Visas and red tape

Citizens and permanent residents of the US, Canada, the UK, Ireland, Australia and all EU countries don't need a visa when visiting the Dominican Republic, but must obtain a ninety-day Dominican Republic tourist card for US$10 (US dollars only) at the airport on arrival; check first with your airline to see if the price of the tourist card is included in your flight. New Zealanders must apply to the Dominican consulate in Sydney for an A$80 visa, valid for up to sixty days' stay. Keep your card on you at all times; if you're asked for it and can't produce it, you may well be detained and fined, though some police officers (but not immigration officers) may ask you instead for a small bribe. A word of warning: foreign passports are a valuable commodity in the Dominican Republic, and passport thefts do occur. Make sure you keep a photocopy in a safe place. When you leave the country, you'll be required to pay a US$10 departure tax (also US dollars only).

and articles on the Cordillera Central and climbing Pico Duarte, along with links to Cabarete businesses and a roundup of Iguana Mama's extensive list of adventure tours.
ⓦ**www.listindiario.com** Online version of the DR's most venerable newspaper; good live music listings.

ⓦ**www.paginasamarillas.com.do**
Yellow Pages covering the entire country.
ⓦ**www.roughguides.com** Log on to the Rough Guides website for DR travel info and highlights and a message board with up-to-the-minute, first-hand accounts of Dominican travel.

Transport and tours

Excellent, inexpensive buses, equipped with plenty of luggage room, service much of the country. Aside from the quality of the movies screened on cross-country rides, trips are relatively pleasant and hassle-free. Even more extensive (and less expensive) is the informal network of guaguas – ranging from fairly decent minibuses to battered, overcrowded vans – that cover every inch of the DR. In most cases, however, you should be prepared for some discomfort – and you'll have a hard time fitting in much luggage, as every square inch of space is packed with passengers. The most heavily populated routes are along the Autopista Duarte between Santo Domingo and Puerto Plata, and the oceanfront highways on the northern and southern coasts.

By bus

Santo Domingo and Santiago are the major hubs for **bus travel,** and some companies do little more than shuttle between the two.
Caribe Tours (☎221-4422, ⓦwww .caribetours.com.do) boasts by far the most extensive network – with connections to Cibao, the Samaná Peninsula, the Barahona region, the entire Northeast Coast and even Port-au-Prince, Haiti – while **Metro** (☎566-7126) can get you from the capital to Cibao, Puerto Plata and the Samaná Peninsula. In addition to these two, you'll find several regional bus companies, though vehicles and drivers tend to vary more in quality. Unless it's a public holiday, you won't need advance **reservations**, but you should arrive at least an hour before departure to be sure of getting a seat.
Fares are extremely cheap: even a cross-country trip from Santo Domingo to Samaná or Monte Cristi will set you back no more than RD$70, while shorter trips fall in the RD$40–50 range. Make sure that the date and time are correct on your ticket; even if the mistake isn't yours, you

cannot normally change your ticket or get a refund.

Public transport

The formal bus companies are great for shuttling back and forth between the major towns, but to head further out into the countryside you're better off trying the informal system of **guaguas**. Guagua routes interlace the entire country (even the most remote areas); in the Southeast and other parts of the country not serviced by Caribe Tours and Metro, they're the best option. That said, most guaguas are not all that comfortable, and you'll have a much less stressful ride if you speak a little Spanish, as English is not widely spoken by the Dominican masses that use and maintain this transport system. To catch a guagua, either ask for the local station or simply stand by the side of the road and wave your arms as it passes. For longer trips, you'll often have to transfer at major towns, but even the longest leg of the trip will cost no more than RD$60; more often, you'll be paying RD$20–40. Be aware, though, that attempted rip-offs of tourists are not unheard of. Ask around and find out the **cost** of a given ride before flagging one down, then clamber onto the vehicle and hand over your money immediately without saying a word. If the *cobrador* (faretaker) won't take the money, get out and wait for the next. Keep a careful eye on the road as you go; you'll have to shout for the driver to pull over when you want to get out.
Though vans serve as the most prevalent type of guagua, you'll find other manifestations as well. Routes leading from Santo Domingo to the Southeast and the Barahona region are often covered by far more comfortable, air-conditioned **minibuses**; along the Northeast Coast, vans are augmented by private cars called **públicos**, which charge RD$5–10 and only go to

the next nearest town and wait to fill up before heading off. *Públicos* also make up part of the **city transport** system in Santo Domingo, and dominate it in Santiago. In Puerto Plata and other, smaller, towns, city transport is instead in the form of **motoconchos**, inexpensive, small-engined motorbikes that ferry you from place to place; they're faster than *públicos* but can be dangerous.

By taxi

Taxis are far more comfortable than other modes of public transport and by foreign standards, a relatively cheap way to travel. You'll usually get better rates if you book a taxi in advance, rather than climbing into one at a designated point. It's also possible to hire a taxi for cross-country travel, though this usually costs even more than car rental. At designated pick-up points within airports and towns, there's always a board listing the established rates for travel to various towns across the country.

By car

Car rental is expensive in the DR, though you can cut costs – and avoid a lot of hassle – by booking in advance with an international operator like Hertz, Dollar or Budget. Recognized international firms, along with reputable Dominican agencies Honda and Nelly, are preferable as they're no more expensive and far less likely to rip you off. Rates start at around US$50–55 per day, with unlimited mileage but no discount for longer rental periods; you should also get full collision insurance, which will be an extra US$10–15 per day. Even with collision, you're contractually responsible for any damage up to RD$25,000. You should therefore take special care to note all dents, scratches and missing parts before signing off; nor should you sign the contract if a total price, including all hidden charges, taxes and fees, is not filled out. Anticipate also high **petrol** costs, which float around RD$100 per gallon. Most pet-

rol stations close around 8pm – and there are none whatsoever in the most remote regions – so keep a careful eye on your tank. If all else fails, look for one of the many roadside tables that sell individual litres of petrol for around RD$50.

Because of the poor quality of many roads, flat tyres are a common occurrence; fortunately, every town has at least one *gomero*, independent tyre shops that do great work for as little as RD$50.

Tours

Various local companies offer island-wide sightseeing tours, either to a set itinerary or customized to your needs. Remember to check whether the price includes entrance fees to attractions. Your hotel may also organize tours.

Tour companies

Iguana Mama ☎571-0908 or 1-800/849-4720, ☎571-0734, ☜www.iguanamama.com. The very best of the country's adventure operators, with imaginative tours, well-trained, friendly and informative staff and an enviable ethical eco-tourism record. They offer a huge selection of US$40–85 mountain-bike day-trips, as well as week-long bike tours of the island, hikes up Mount Isabela (see p.112) and multi-day treks through the Cordillera Central to Pico Duarte (see p.145). They also rent quality mountain bikes for US$25/day, and do horseback riding for US$25/half day.
Tody Tours ☎686-0882, ☜www.todytours.com. One-, three- and five-day birding excursions with 4WD into the Dominican wilderness at Parques Nacionales del Este, Bermúdez, Bahoruco and Jaragua. The price is steep at $150/day plus expenses, but the quality is high.
Tours, Trips, Treks, and Travel ☎867-8884, ☜www.4tdomrep.com. An array of adventure sports and culture tours – from kiteboarding to mountain climbing – run by top-notch guides.

Money

The Dominican Republic is one of the last true budget destinations in the Caribbean; only neighbouring Haiti is cheaper. Package deals at quality Dominican all-inclusives are relatively low-priced, and in many parts of the country shoestring travellers can spend as little as US$40/£21 per day.

Currency

Two distinct economies operate within the Dominican Republic – the **US dollar** economy of all-inclusive hotels and tour operators and that of the official Dominican currency, the **peso** (RD$). Throughout most of the country, you'll have to change any foreign currency into pesos in order to conduct transactions. At the all-inclusive resorts and other foreign-owned tourism companies, though, all prices will be quoted in US dollars, and Dominican pesos are accepted reluctantly – and at a poor rate.

Pesos come in notes of 5, 10, 20, 50, 100, 500, 1000 and 5000; there are also 0.10, 0.25, 0.50 and 1 peso coins, though only the last sees much use these days. Today the peso floats freely against the dollar, which means that there's some variation in exchange rate from day to day; it hovered at 30 pesos to the US dollar at the time this book went to press.

Costs

The Dominican Republic can be incredibly cheap if you stick to the smaller hotels and get around using public transport. With the exception of Santo Domingo you'll have no problem finding some sort of modest but decent **accommodation** for US$20 or less and a **meal** at a Dominican comedor will set you back no more than US$2.50, while nicer restaurants range US$10–35 per person. Especially cheap are the **buses and guaguas**; the former can get you from one end of the country to the other for US$4 or less, the latter for under US$2.50. At **resort towns** like Cabarete and Boca Chica, prices are more inflated. **All-inclusive** hotel guests should be sure to bring some cash, as the quality of many hotel restaurants is not outstanding and you'll

enjoy your trip more if you get out of your resort complex.

Changing money

Banks offer the best exchange rates; keep your receipts, as this allows you to exchange thirty percent of the pesos back into hard currency on departure. In a pinch, smaller casas de cambio, which usually offer only slightly worse rates, are fine, though you should avoid the street moneychangers you'll see in most cities, as counterfeit pesos and sleight-of-hand rip-offs are standard practice.

Travellers' cheques, credit and cash cards

Travellers' cheques are undeniably a safe way to keep your money, but aside from large hotels, car rental firms and pricey restaurants, most Dominican businesses don't accept them. Travellers' cheques in US dollars are preferable, though banks and most hotels will cash cheques in European currencies as well.

Credit cards come in handy as a backup source of funds, and are accepted by most mid-range and all expensive hotels, as well as many restaurants – though of course in smaller towns and rural areas they will be slightly less helpful. Your **cash cards** from home will also come in handy, as almost all sizeable towns and resorts (outside of the more rural parts of the country) have **ATMs** that allow you to withdraw cash directly from your bank account. Indeed, your cash or ATM card is by far the safest and most convenient way to manage your money while travelling. Keep in mind, though, that many local banks charge a fee in addition to the fee charged by your home bank, which can add up to US$4 per transaction.

Accommodation

The Dominican Republic has become the most popular destination in the Caribbean thanks to its preponderance of all-inclusive hotels, which make package vacations here far cheaper than elsewhere. The all-inclusives do have their downsides: the food is usually mediocre, and you'll be stuck in a walled-off complex for your entire trip, which can get claustrophobic. Plenty of other options exist for travellers who want

to get out and see the country: luxury high-rise resorts along the capital's Malecón, independently operated beach hotels, rooms for rent in Dominican family homes, and an assortment of bearable budget hotels, many with private bath, hot water and a/c. Away from the main tourist spots you can expect to pay around US$20–40 for the night; in resort towns prices rise to US$40–100. Reservations are essential

Accommodation prices

The accommodation prices in the Guide refer to the cost per night of the least expensive double room during the winter, or high, season (mid-Dec to mid-April). Room prices on the island are usually quoted in US dollars, and we have followed this practice in the Guide. Nearly every hotel has a significant difference between its winter and summer prices, with summer prices lower by as much as 25 percent. With the all-inclusives, bear in mind that if you book for a week or more, particularly as part of a package, prices will normally be much lower.

for the all-inclusives, where you'll get up to 75 percent off the price by booking with a travel agent as part of a package before you arrive. In the major resort towns most independent hotels require reservations for the high season, but in the rest of the country they're not necessary.

Independent hotels and pensiones

When travelling, most Dominicans stay at the spartan **budget hotels** that you'll find dotted throughout the country. If you do likewise you'll save a lot of money, but you often get what you pay for: fairly nondescript, box-like rooms, best avoided except for sleep. Some of them have shared bath, many more cold-water showers. Look to spend around US$20 for these establishments. It's easy to mistake the many roadside **cabañas turísticas** for budget traveller hotels; in fact these hotels charge hourly, and are mainly used by local couples.

Traditional **pensiones** can still be found in many towns, though over the past two decades they've begun to die out. These rooms within a private Dominican home offer an excellent opportunity for contact with local people. Pensiones vary widely in quality, so take a good look at your room before deciding. Nicer, **mid-range hotels**

are available in areas regularly frequented by foreigners. Ranging between US$35 and US$65, they feature a/c, strong hot water and more pleasant rooms. Hotels at the lower end of this price range are often especially good value; at the higher end you'll get a few luxuries thrown in, like cable TV or breakfast. If there's one around and you can afford it, consider the independent **luxury hotels** as well, which usually charge US$80–150. The majority are clustered in Santo Domingo, but you'll also find at least one in most big cities and a couple along the rural coast. You can often get better rates (up to 30 percent off) at these hotels on weekends, as they cater mostly to business travellers.

All-inclusives

The Dominican Republic is the archetypal, high-volume all-inclusive destination, where a single price covers your room, all meals and drinks, and a variety of activities. If you go all-inclusive, you should do so through a **package** arranged by a travel agent in your home country. All-inclusives, usually stationed right on prime beachfront, can offer a wonderful, peaceful beach vacation in relative luxury, and despite a blanket no-tips policy, the staff are generally pleasant and accommodating.

Communications

It's easy to keep in touch with home by phone, fax or email while you're in the DR. Storefront phone centres are scattered about the country, though the price can be steep. Internet cafés are a booming business in the major cities and resort areas, but you'll have a hard time finding a connection out in the campos. Postal mail

is slower, less efficient and not guaranteed to arrive.

Phones

The DR has several **private telephone companies**, all of which operate phone centres in Dominican towns and villages.

Dialling codes

To call the Dominican Republic from abroad, dial your international access code (see below) + 809 + seven-digit number.

UK ☏001	Australia ☏0011
USA ☏011	New Zealand ☏00
Canada ☏011	

To call abroad from the Dominican Republic, dial 00 + country code (see below) + area code minus first 0 + number

UK ☏44	Australia ☏61
USA ☏1	New Zealand ☏64
Canada ☏1	

The oldest and most dependable is **Verizon**, which charges RD$17 per minute to North America; RD$25 per minute to Europe; and RD$35 per minute to Australia and New Zealand. Another option is to purchase a Verizon calling card, sold at Verizon phone centres and most *bodegas* in various denominations. The charge is RD$10 per minute to North America, RD$25 per minute to Europe. These are especially handy when calling from a hotel room; most long-distance charges from your room are exorbitant, but if you use a Verizon card they'll simply charge you the price of a local call. Within the DR, you must always dial the country-wide area code of 1-809, before the seven-digit number.

Internet

Verizon has Internet connections in its many phone centres; there's typically one in every town. You can also opt for one of the hundreds of Internet cafés that have sprung up in major cities and resort areas. Rates vary, but are generally around RD$1/minute; make sure they have at least a DSL connection. Most all-inclusives offer free Internet access to their guests, though you're usually limited to twenty minutes or so per visit due to high demand.

Mail

Dominican *correos*, or post offices, are notoriously slow; even if you use **special delivery** (highly recommended) you still have to allow at least three weeks for your postcard or letter to reach North America, and at least a month for it to reach Europe or Australasia. Postage costs RD$3 to North America, RD$4 elsewhere. The most convenient way to **receive mail** is to have it sent to your hotel, though most post offices have a reasonably reliable *lista de correos*, where mail is held for you for up to four weeks, at a charge of RD$10 per letter. Bring your passport (or a photocopy) when picking up mail.

Food and drink

If you take all your meals at an all-inclusive hotel, you'll get little sense of how Dominicans eat and drink; the bland "international" buffet fare and watered-down daiquiris just can't compete with the delicious, no-nonsense, high-quality cooking at the many local restaurants, or the rum drinks on offer just outside the compound walls.

Eating

Dominicans call their cuisine *comida criolla*, and it's a delicious – if a bit greasy – blend of Spanish, African and Taino elements, with interesting regional variants across the island. Dishes usually include rice and beans – referred to locally as *la bandera dominicana* (the Dominican flag) – using either *habichuelas* (red beans) or tiny black peas known as *morros*. Most often the rice is supplemented with chicken, either fried, grilled or served *asopao* (in a rich, soupy sauce). Invariably main courses come with *plátanos* (deep-fried green plantains) and a small coleslaw salad.

Local **breakfasts** typically include *huevos revueltos* (scrambled eggs), sometimes *con jamón* (with bits of ham); *mangú*, mashed plantains mixed with oil and fried onion; *queso frito*, a deep-fried cheese; *jugo de naranja* (orange juice; also called *jugo de china* in the Southwest); and a strong cup of coffee, either *solo* or *con leche*, but always with a healthy dose of sugar.

Lunches are hearty, too, and generally consumed between noon and 2pm. But **dinner** is the day's main meal, and is almost always a family affair. Aside from the omnipresent chicken, popular main courses include *mondongo*, a tripe stew strictly for the strong of stomach; *mofongo*, a tasty blend of plantains, pork rinds and garlic; and *bistec encebollado*, grilled steak topped with onions and peppers. **Special occasions** call for either *chivo* (roast goat) with *cassava*, a crispy, flat bread inherited from the Tainos, made with ground yucca roots; or *sancocho*, considered the national delicacy, a hearty stew with five different kinds of meat, four types of tuber, and a bewildering array of vegetables and spices. For the best in Dominican eating, go for the **seafood**, which is traditionally prepared one of five ways: **criolla**, in a flavourful, slightly spicy tomato sauce; *al ajillo*, doused in a rich garlic sauce; *al horno*, roasted with lemon; *al orégano*, in a tangy sauce with fresh oregano and heavy cream; and *con coco*, in a tomato, garlic and coconut milk blend especially prevalent on the Samaná Peninsula. Local fish to try include *mero* (sea bass), *chillo* (red snapper) and *carite* (kingfish).

Dominican **desserts** are good but extremely sweet; a favorite is *dulces con coco*, made with molasses and coconut shavings. Healthier and even tastier are the tremendous variety of **tropical fruits**. *Guineos* (bananas), *lechoza* (papaya) and *piña* (pineapple) are the most popular, but you won't regret trying the local *limoncillos*, tiny, delicious lime-like fruits sold in bunches, and *chinola*, Dominican passion fruit. The DR is especially known for its mangos; *fresas* (strawberries) are cultivated in the Constanza region and grow wild in the Sierra Bahoruco, and so are widely available.

Drinking

Grown in the heights of the Cordillera Central, Dominican coffee is among the best in the world and a major export earner for the country.

Be sure also to sample the fresh coconut milk sold by street vendors and batidas, popular fruit shakes with ice, milk and either papaya, mango, pineapple or banana – freshly made in a comedor, they bear no relation to the cartoned stuff bearing the same name. A similar drink traditionally served in Dominican homes is **morir soñando**, a heavenly concoction of orange juice, condensed milk, sugar and crushed ice. The local brew of MamaJuana, made with rum and tree bark, is said to increase lifespan, and can be found around Sosúa, Cabarete and Puerto Plata. The DR has several beer brands, but by far the best and most popular is Presidente, which is served in both normal-sized and surreally large bottles, and compares favourably with beers from across the world. Dominicans are obsessed with getting it as ice-cold as possible – if you don't want it to be a block of ice when you open it, do as they do and rub your hand under the bottom of the bottle before popping the cap. Also popular are the excellent, inexpensive local **rums**, of which Bermúdez is the very best. In the discos and bars, ask for a *Cuba libre servicio*: a bottle of rum, two Cokes and a bucket of ice.

Sports and leisure

The Dominican Republic's highly lucrative package-tourism industry centres on its endless supply of idyllic, palm-fringed beaches and crystal-clear turquoise waters. Watersports range from swimming, snorkelling, scuba diving, windsurfing and surfing to deep-sea fishing and whale watching.

Though many beaches are protected from powerful ocean currents by natural barriers, others have dangerous riptides, and should be avoided by all but the strongest swimmers; meanwhile, the Caribbean waters off Santo Domingo are shark-infested and should be eschewed by all. Inland, the island's many rivers and lakes are perfect for white-water rafting, waterfall cascading and lake fishing. The country's five separate mountain ranges are popular for mountain biking, horseback riding and trekking. In the resorts you'll also find golf courses, tennis courts and, in La Romana's Casa de Campo, polo grounds.

Snorkelling and scuba diving

The only area where you'll still find a large system of intact coral reefs lies west of Puerto Plata, between La Isabela and Monte Cristi. By no coincidence, this is the most remote coastal region in the country, and devilishly difficult to access for scuba diving and snorkelling. A number of tour operators, however, can take you out to parts of the reef, including Dive Samaná. Along the southern coast, the best snorkelling is in Bahía de Neiba, just east of Barahona, where you may spot manatees; at Isla Catalina, a small, heavily visited island near La Romana where the fish have been known to eat out of snorkellers' hands; at Isla Saona, an enormous mangrove island with decent reefs, just east of Bayahibe; and at Parque Nacional La Caleta just east of Santo Domingo, where the National Parks Department sank a retired treasure-hunting ship called the *Hickory* in 1984, which has since been calcified with new reef that is feeding ground for an array of sea creatures. Numerous private operators, and most all-inclusive hotels, offer trips to the reefs, wrecks and caves that dot the Southeast Coast, along with diving instruction. The well-established **Dolphin Dive Center** (☎571-0842, ⊛www.dolphindivecenter .com) offers three-day PADI Open Water scuba-diving instruction for US$319 and a variety of dives on local reefs and wrecks for US$25–40/dive.

Windsurfing, kiteboarding and surfing

The northern resort of Cabarete is the **windsurfing** capital of the Americas and the venue for the Cabarete Race Week and the Encuentra Classic, both major world competitions. If you don't have any windsurfing experience, learning here will be a challenge due to the strength of the waves and wind. Nevertheless, a dozen windsurfing clubs offer equipment rental and high-quality tutoring. Much more appealing for beginners is the burgeoning sport of **kiteboarding**, which takes less time to learn and is truly exhilarating – even novices are often shot up in the air by their kites as they skate on the waves. Along the country's southern coast, scenic beach town Las Salinas has quietly become a windsurfing

centre as well, with milder conditions and a small windsurfing centre that's used mostly by wealthy Dominicans.

Surfing is less organized and mostly done by locals. Though you won't find any surfing schools, popular venues include Playa Encuentra near Cabarete and Playas Grande and Preciosa just east of Río San Juan. Be aware, though, that these are challenging spots for the sport, and most have no posted lifeguard; they should only be used by those with a good deal of experience.

Cabarete watersports schools and equipment rental

Carib Bic Center ☎571-0640, ℻571-0649, ⊛www.caribwind.com. Slick outfit, with a great equipment shop and a well-trained, friendly staff.

Dive Samaná ☎538-0020. Las Galeras dive school that runs trips to the reef and caves.

Fanatic ☎ & ℻571-0861, ⊛www .fanatic-cabarete.com. Quality operation that offers lots of personal attention. Also has a beach bar with tasty cocktails.

Kite Excite ☎571-9509, ⊛www.kite-excite.com. One of the original kiteboard schools; German-run but mostly Dominican staff.

Laurel Eastman Kiteboard Center Aparthotel Caracol ☎571-0564, ⊛www .laureleastman.com. Founded by a legendary female kiteboarder, this school does the best job training newbies.

Vela/Spinout/Dare2Fly ☎571-0805, ℻571-0856, ⊛www.velacabarete.com. German-owned and the best-stocked of Cabarete's windsurf centres with free daily clinics and a lively social scene. The small, relaxing bar offers great lunches.

Sailing, fishing and whale watching

The DR is a major port of call for Caribbean sailors, with marinas in Luperón, Manzanillo and Samaná. Luperón is the most popular, and thus the best place to hire a boat for a day-trip along the island's northern coast. Check in at the Luperón Marina (which has no telephone) a day in advance to arrange a trip.

Many of the all-inclusive resorts feature daily **deep-sea fishing** tours that run around RD$1500 per day; standard catches include sea bass, red snapper and kingfish, though you can also hook good game fish, from wahoo and porpoise to marlin, on tours along the Southeast Coast. On the Northwest Coast between Monte Cristi and Luperón, the reef makes for some excellent fishing; expect to catch wahoo, king mackerel and dorado year-round, with lots of tuna June–Aug, blue marlin May–Sept, white marlin Aug–Oct and sailfish Nov–April.

Every winter, over four thousand **humpback whales** from across the Atlantic come to the Bahía de Samaná and Silver Banks Sanctuary to mate, give birth and nurse infants. High season is January and February, with some early arrivals in December and a number of hangers-on in March. Whale-watching boats set out from the city of Samaná every day in high season.

Whale-watching tour operators

Aquatic Adventures ☎305/827-0211, ℗827-0212, ⊛www.aquaticadventures .com. Texas-based eco-tour outfit that offers US$2200 week-long whale-watching cruises in the Silver Banks Sanctuary, departing from Puerto Plata.
Victoria Marine ☎538-2494, ⊛www. whalesamana.com. The company that started whale watching in the Samaná Bay, and still the best whale-tour operator in the entire Caribbean. Boats go out thrice daily in whale season (mid-December through February) to get an up-close look at hundreds of humpbacks as they frolic, flirt and give birth to their young along the Northeast Coast.

River sports

Mountain resort Jarabacoa, deep in the heart of the Cordillera Central, is a hub for **white-water rafting** and **kayaking**. Several tour operators with experienced guides run daily trips down the turbulent Río Yaque del Norte. Expect a moderately challenging trip with several tricky twists and turns and a couple of steep drops. You can also spend as long as a week kayaking through the Cordillera Central rivers on organized excursions.

Jarabacoa, Cabarete and Las Terrenas also have terrific opportunities for **cascading** (descending a rock face on elastic cords) down various waterfalls as high as 75m, which when accompanied by experienced guides is far less dangerous than it sounds, but undoubtedly exhilarating. The best of the tour operators that does fresh-water trips is Rancho Baiguate, but you can also book through Franz's Aventuras del Caribe or Iguana Mama (see p.167).

River-tour operators

Franz's Aventuras del Caribe ☎242-0395, ℗223-6886, ⊛www.hispaniola .com/whitewater. Top of the bunch when it comes to white-water adrenaline rushes, Franz's stick to what they know best – rivers. Basic rafting trips on the Yaque del Norte start from as little as US$40, and they also offer kayaking, including beginners' courses and expert descents of local rivers (starting at US$65/day).
Get Wet ☎586 1170, ℗ranchobaiguate @verizon.net.do. Rancho Baiguate–operated by a qualified mountain guide who offers canyoning (walking, swimming and rappelling down a mountain river) trips in the surrounding mountains. Another great feature is their Tropical Wakeboard Center, which does water-skiing and wakeboarding (water-skiing on a miniature surfboard) along the Río Yasica (US$120/ full day). The scenery is stunning and the adventure unbeatable.

Mountain sports

The island's mountain ranges afford infinite possibilities for **mountain biking**. Cabarete's Iguana Mama (see p.167) is the country's major mountain-bike tour outfit, with challenging day-trips into the Cordillera Septentrional and week-long mountain-bike and camping excursions from one end of the island to the other. They also offer **bike rental**, with well-serviced Cannondales for US$20/day. The best **hiking** is along five separate trails that lead from disparate parts of the Cordillera Central to Pico Duarte, the highest peak in the Caribbean; hikes usually range from three to six days. **Horseback-riding** excursions are also quite popular. In addition to the plethora of outfits that offer day-rides along the country's beaches, you'll find quality mountain-riding operators in Cabarete, Punta Cana, Las Terrenas, Jarabacoa, San José de las Matas and Río San Juan.

Mountain-sports operators

Rancho Baiguate ☎ 574-4940, ⊛www .ranchobaiguate.com. Mountain-sports specialist that offers daily first-rate white-water rafting, waterfall rappelling and mountain-trekking excursions from their

base in Jarabacoa. Excellent accommodation, comfortable camping on multi-day
mountain hikes, and a truly smooth and
professional operation.
Rancho Marabel ☎253-0954, ✆www
.hispaniola.com/alcantara. A large horse
ranch in the mountains near Cabarete;
rides cost US$60 for a full day, including
a trip to an especially beautiful waterfall
where you can risk life and limb by jumping
off it into a deep natural pool.

Caving

Caving through one of the island's extensive systems, many bearing Taino rock art,
makes for a memorable adventure. Among
the easiest are the coastal caves in Parque
Nacional Los Haitises, accessible by boat
tour, but the most rewarding are the Taino
caves in Parque Nacional del Este near

Bayahibe, where Taino art references to
Christopher Columbus and the early
Spaniards have recently been discovered.
Other prime places for exploration include
caves near San Cristóbal, Monción, Caba-
rete, Las Galeras and Boca de Yuma.

Golf

Three golf courses stand head and shoulders above the rest: the Pete Dye–designed
Teeth of the Dog course at Casa de Campo
in La Romana (☎523-8800), and the
excellent Robert Trent Jones courses at
Playa Dorada (☎372-6020) and Playa
Grande (☎563-5565) on the Northeast
Coast. All three have the majority of their
holes set on spectacular open oceanfront
and are occasionally used as tournament
venues. Greens fees typically run around
US$65 for 18 holes.

Festivals

The Dominican Republic has a bewildering barrage of festivals. On every day of
the year, there seems to be some kind of
celebration somewhere. The majority are
regional fiestas patronales, held in honour
of the city or town's patron saint, who is
often syncretized to an African god.

January 1
Guloya Festival The famous mummers of
San Pedro de Macorís run a morning pro-
cession through the streets of San Pedro's
Miramar barrio.

January 21
Virgen de Altagracia By far the most
important religious day on the Dominican
calendar, a prayer-of-intercession day to
the country's patron.

February
Carnival The pre-eminent celebration of
the year, held on every Sunday in February.
La Vega and Santo Domingo are your best
bets; in Monte Cristi the festivities can get
violent, while San Cristóbal holds a populist
festival with a definite political edge.

March/April
Semana Santa The Christian Holy Week
is also the most important week of Haitian

and Dominican *vodú*. Traditional *gagá*
festivals take place in and around the
southwestern town of Cabral, among other
locations.

Espíritu Santo In honour of the Holy Spirit,
syncretized to the Congo region's supreme
deity Kalunda. Huge celebrations in various
towns; occurs seven weeks after Semana
Santa.

May 3
San Felipe A boisterous cultural celebration on Puerto Plata's Malecón, with lots
of live music.

June 13
San Antonio Fiesta patronales in Bonao
and Sosúa.

June 17–24
San Juan Bautista A religious festival in
Baní, run by a brotherhood dating from the
Haitian occupation; they perform a distinc-
tive style of music called sarandunga.

June 29
San Pedro Apostol A magnificent Cocolo
festival in San Pedro de Macorís, with
roving bands of guloyas performing dance
dramas on the street.

July
Merengue Festival An outdoor music festival on Santo Domingo's Malecón and Plaza España, with virtually every famous merengue act from the last forty years.

August 16
Restoration Day Nationwide celebration of independence from Spain, with large parties in Santiago and Santo Domingo.

September 29
San Miguel After the Virgin de Altagracia, San Miguel is the most important Dominican saint, with major festivals across the country.

October (third week)
Merengue Festival A popular music festival in Puerto Plata, with big acts playing all over town and lots of partying on the Malecón. Date varies from year to year.

December 4
Santa Bárbara Fiesta patronal for the city of Samaná, including a procession that features the music of Doña Bertilia, Queen of the Bamboulá, a popular music on the peninsula.

Directory

Banks Typically Mon–Fri 9am–12.30pm & 2–5pm, Sat 9am–12.30pm.

Children Most families stick to the all-inclusive resorts, which generally have good childcare facilities and plenty of diversions for kids. Regardless, make sure that your children use a heavy sun block (at least SPF25) and brush their teeth with bottled water. Officially, children who are accompanied by only one of their parents may remain in the country for no more than thirty days. Children travelling without parents must have a notarized permit from their home country's Dominican consulate.

Disabled travellers There are unfortunately few facilities for disabled travellers, and no rental cars come with hand controls. Some major monuments, however, have ramps and most all-inclusives offer wheelchair access to certain rooms and all of their restaurants, casinos, bars and beaches.

Dress Dominican society is fairly formal, and a lot of emphasis is placed on personal appearance, with women wearing long skirts and men trousers and shirtsleeves even in August. If you're on the street wearing shorts during the day, you'll simply be regarded as a typical tourist (to which no stigma is attached) but those who are scruffy, unshaven or dressed like backpackers will be looked down upon. To visit many of the sights in Santo Domingo – for example, the Cathedral and the Altar de la Patria – men will have to wear trousers and women long skirts (below the knee).

Electricity 110 volts AC, like in US and Canada. Plugs are standard American two-pins, so European visitors should bring suitable adaptors. Intermittent power outages throughout the country mean that you should make sure your hotel has a generator that they're willing to use 24 hours a day.

Emergencies Dial ☎911 in case of emergency. Quality medical facilities include Santo Domingo: Clínica Abreu, Beller 42 ☎688-4411; Puerto Plata: Clínica Brugal, Ariza 15 and Kennedy; Cabarete: Servi-Med, Carretera 5 at town centre; Santiago: Centro Médico Cibao, Calle Duarte just west of Las Carreras.

Laundry Santo Domingo: Lavaseco, Independencia 208; Las Terrenas: Lavendería P&M, Calle Carmen; Sosúa: Josefina, Plaza Colonial, Calle Alejandro Martínez; Santiago: Joseph Cleaners, Las Carreras and Sabana Larga.

Pharmacies Santo Domingo: Carol, Ricard 24; Las Terrenas: Farmacentro Principal, Calle Duarte; Puerto Plata: Superfarmacia Metropolis, Beller 129; Santiago: Farmacia San Luis, San Luis 61 and Independencia.

Police ☎911.

Time The Dominican Republic is in North America's Eastern Standard Time Zone (same time as New York and Atlanta) and 5 hours behind GMT.

Tipping Most restaurants add on a ten percent service charge, but this is rarely given to the waiting staff. It's customary to give service staff an additional ten percent. Most all-inclusive hotels, however, have a no-tip policy.

Toilets You'll notice a definite lack of public toilets in the DR, and the ones in modest restaurants and petrol stations are often without seats. With the exception of the all-inclusive hotels, you should not put toilet paper down the toilet. The sewage system is not equipped to deal with the paper, and you'll only create a blockage. There's always a receptacle provided for the paper next to the toilet.

Language

Spanish

English is spoken in the main tourist areas, but you'll get a far better reception if you try communicating with Dominicans in their native Spanish tongue, and you'll be helped everywhere by people who are eager to try and understand even the most faltering attempt. For more than a brief introduction to the language, pick up the *Rough Guide Spanish Dictionary Phrasebook*.

Pronunciation

The rules of Dominican Spanish pronunciation are pretty straightforward and strictly observed.

A   somewhere between the A sound in "back" and that in "father".
E   as in "get".
I   as in "police".
O   as in "hot".
U   as in "rule".
C   is soft before E and I, hard otherwise: *cerca* is pronounced "serka".
G   works the same way: a guttural H sound (like the *ch* in "loch") before E or I, a hard G elsewhere: *gigante* becomes "higante".
H   is always silent.
J   is the same sound as guttural G: *jamón* is pronounced "hamón".
LL is pronounced as a Y at the beginning of a word, a soft J elsewhere: *llama* is pronounced "yama", but *ballena* (whale) becomes "bajzhena" instead of "bayena".
N   is as in English, unless it has a tilde accent over it, when it becomes NY: *mañana* sounds like "manyana".
QU is pronounced like the English K.
R   is rolled, RR doubly so.
V   sounds more like B, *vino* becoming "beano".
Z   is the same as the soft C: *cerveza* is thus "serbesa".

Words and phrases

Basics

yes, no	sí, no	open, closed	abierto/a, cerrado/a
please, thank you	por favor, gracias	with, without	con, sin
where, when	dónde, cuando	good, bad	bueno/a, malo/a
what, how much	qué, cuanto	big, small	grande, pequeño/a
here, there	aquí, allí	more, less	más, menos
this, that	este, eso	today, tomorrow	hoy, mañana
now, later	ahora, más tarde	yesterday	ayer

LANGAUGE

Words and phrases

Greetings and reponses

Hello, goodbye	Hola, adiós
Good morning	Buenos días
Good afternoon/ night	Buenas tardes/ noches
See you later	Hasta luego
Sorry	Lo siento
Excuse me	Con permiso/perdón
How are you?	¿Como está?
I (don't) understand	(No) Entiendo
Not at all/you're welcome	De nada
Do you speak English?	¿Habla inglés?
I don't speak Spanish	No hablo español
My name is . . .	Me llamo . . .
What is your name?	¿Como se llama usted?
I am English	Soy inglés(a)
. . . American	. . . americano/a
. . . Australian	. . . australiano/a
. . . Canadian	. . . canadiense/a
. . . Irish	. . . irlandés(a)
. . . Scottish	. . . escosés(a)
. . . Welsh	. . . galés(a)
. . . New Zealander	. . . neozelandés(a)

Accommodation, transport and directions

I want	Quiero
I'd like	Quisiera
Do you know . . . ?	¿Sabe . . . ?
I don't know	No sé
There is (is there?)	(¿) Hay (?)
Give me . . .	Deme . . .
(one like that)	(uno así)
Do you have . . . ?	¿Tiene . . . ?
. . . the time	. . . la hora
. . . a room	. . . un habitación
. . . with two beds	. . . con dos camas
. . . with a double bed	. . . con una cama matrimonial
It's for one person	Es para una persona
. . . two people	. . . dos personas
. . . for one night (one week)	. . . para una noche (una semana)
It's fine, how much is it?	¿Está bien, cuánto es?
Can one . . . ?	¿Se puede . . . ?
. . . camp near here?	¿ . . . acampar aquí (cerca)?
Is there a hotel nearby?	¿Hay un hotel aquí?
How do I get to . . . ?	¿Por dónde se va a . . . ?
Left, right	Izquierda, derecha
Straight on	Derecho, siga

Where is . . . ?	¿Dónde está . . . ?
. . . the bus station	. . . el estación de autobuses?
. . . the nearest bank	. . . el banco más cercano?
. . . the post office	. . . el correo?
. . . the toilet	. . . el baño?
Where does the bus to . . . leave from?	¿De dónde sale el autobus para...?
I'd like a (return) ticket to . . .	Quisiera un tiquete (de ida y vuelta) para . . .
What time does it leave (arrive in . . .)?	¿A qué hora sale (llega en . . .)?
What's that?	¿Qué es eso?

Numbers and days

1	un/uno/una
2	dos
3	tres
4	cuatro
5	cinco
6	seis
7	siete
8	ocho
9	nueve
10	diez
11	once
12	doce
13	trece
14	catorce
15	quince
16	dieciséis
20	veinte
21	veintiuno
30	treinta
40	cuarenta
50	cincuenta
60	sesenta
70	setenta
80	ochenta
90	noventa
100	cien(to)
101	ciento uno
200	doscientos
201	doscientos uno
500	quinientos
1000	mil
2000	dos mil
2001	dos mil uno
first	primero/a
second	segundo/a
third	tercero/a
Monday	lunes
Tuesday	martes
Wednesday	miércoles
Thursday	jueves
Friday	viernes
Saturday	sábado
Sunday	domingo

Menu reader

Basics

¿Hay?…	Do you have? (Is there…?)
Un menú, por favor	A menu, please
La cuenta, por favor	The bill, please
Quiero…	I would like…
Soy vegetariano/a	I'm a vegetarian
Sin carne	Without meat
Dos cervezas	Two beers
Salud!	Cheers!
Pan	Bread
Pan de cassava	Cassava bread
Arroz	Rice
Mantequilla	Butter
Queso típico	white Dominican cheese
Queso frito	Fried cheese
Sal	Salt
Pimienta	Pepper
Azúcar	Sugar
Sin azúcar	Without sugar
Huevos	Eggs

Cooking terms

Al ajillo	Garlic sauce
Barbacoa	Barbecued
Al carbón	Grilled
Criolla	Tomato-based creole sauce
Frito	Fried
Al horno	Roasted

Soups and salads

Ensalada campesina	Watercress, tomatoes, oregano and radishes
Ensalada típica	Shredded cabbage and carrots with oil and vinegar
Ensalada verde	Green salad
Mondongo	Tripe stew
Sancocho	Stew with several kinds of meat, tubers and an array of spices
Sopa de guandules	Pigeon pea soup
Sopa haitiana	Bone marrow soup
Sopa de morros	Black bean and rice soup
Sopa pescado	Fish soup
Sopa de pollo con fideos	Chicken noodle soup
Sopa verdura	Vegetable soup

Meat

Bistec	Beefsteak
Bistec encebollado	Beefsteak with onions
Carne ripiada	Shredded beef
Chicarrones	Fried bits of pork or chicken
Chivo	Goat
Chuletas de puerco	Pork chops
Conejo	Rabbit
Empanadas	Ground-beef-filled pastries
Guinea	Guinea hen
Jamón	Ham
Longaniza	Spicy sausage made from tripe, ground pork, garlic and oregano
Mofongo	Pork rinds, plantains and garlic
Parrillada	Argentine-style meat platter
Patitas de puerco	Pig's feet
Pollo al carbón	Grilled chicken
Pollo asopao	Chicken and rice served in a rich, creamy sauce
Pollo frito	Fried chicken
Puerco	Pork

Seafood

Atún	Tuna
Calamar	Squid
Camarones	Shrimp
Cangrejo	Crab
Carite	Kingfish
Chillo	Red snapper
Lambí	Conch
Langosta	Clawless lobster
Mariscos	Seafood
Mero	Sea bass
Pulpo	Octopus

Fruits and vegetables

Aguacate	Avocado
Chinola	Passion fruit
Fresas	Strawberries
Guineo	Banana
Lechoza	Papaya
Limón	Lemon
Limoncillo	Tiny, lime-like fruits with tasty pulp
Mango	Mango
Naranja, China	Orange
Piña	Pineapple
Tamarindo	Tamarind

Zapote	Egg-shaped fruit with brown skin and sweet red pulp
Batata	Sweet potato
Cassava	Yucca
Cebolla	Onion
Habichuelas	Red beans
Maiz	Corn
Mangú	Mashed plantains with onions and oil
Morros	Black peas and rice
Ñame	An indigenous tuber that's a popular alternative to potatoes
Palmito	Heart of palm
Papa	Potato
Papas fritas	French fries
Plátano	Plantain
Tostones	Double-fried plantains

Desserts

Arroz con leche	Rice pudding
Dulce con coco	Coconut sweet
Dulce de batata	Sweet-potato dessert

Dulce de leche	Milk sweet
Dulce de naranja	Orange marmalade sweet
Helado	Ice cream
Pudin de pan	Bread pudding

Drinks

Agua	Water
Agua purificada	Purified water
Batida	Fruit shake with pulp
Café con leche	Coffee with hot milk
Café solo	Black coffee
Cerveza	Beer
Cuba libre	Rum and Coke
Jugo	Juice
Jugo de naranja, jugo de china	Orange juice
Leche	Milk
Limonada	Lemonade
Mama Juana	Bark, leaves, honey, rum and wine
Morir soñando	Orange juice, condensed milk and sugar
Refresco	Juice with sugar
Ron	Rum
Vino	Wine

Glossary

apagón power blackout
bachata twangy ballad music, with a steadily emphasized offbeat
balneario swimming hole
la bandera dominicana literally "the Dominican flag", it refers to the national dish of rice and beans.
barrio neighbourhood.
botánica shop where various items related to folk religion can be purchased
campesino rural Dominican peasantry
campo settlement too small to be considered a pueblo
carretera highway
casa de cambio small currency-exchange shop
casa de huespedes also called pensión, a private home with rooms to let to travellers
chin a little bit
club gallístico circular, two-tiered wooden venues for cockfights
colmado Dominican grocery shack.
comedor small, family-run restaurant serving local food

fiesta patronal festival for the patron saint of a town or city
gomero tyre-repair shop
guagua privately owned vans and minibuses that are the primary form of transportation in the DR
Malecón boardwalk avenue along the ocean
merengue the fast-paced national dance music, less rhythmically intricate than salsa, with a repetitive thump right on the beat
motoconcho small-engined motorbikes used for inter-city transport
pensión a private home with rooms to let to travellers
público weather-beaten automobiles used as public transport
pueblo small Dominican town
son the grandfather of today's electrified salsa, with the same rhythmic 3 beat/2 beat pattern, but an emphasis on acoustic instruments

Stay in touch

Rough Guides FREE full-colour newsletter
News, travel issues, music reviews, readers'
letter and the lastest dispatches from authors
on the road

If you would like to receive Rough News, please
send us your name and address:

Rough Guides

80 Strand London
WC2R 0RL

4th Floor, 345
Hudson St, New York
NY10014, USA

newslettersubs@roughguides.co.uk

small print & Index

SMALL PRINT

A Rough Guide to Rough Guides

Dominican Republic DIRECTIONS is published by Rough Guides. The first **Rough Guide to Greece**, published in 1982, was a student scheme that became a publishing phenomenon. The immediate success of the book – with numerous reprints and a Thomas Cook Prize shortlisting – spawned a series that rapidly covered dozens of destinations. Rough Guides had a ready market among low-budget backpackers, but soon also acquired a much broader and older readership that relished Rough Guides' wit and inquisitiveness as much as their enthusiastic, critical approach. Everyone wants value for money, but not at any price. Rough Guides soon began supplementing the "rougher" information about hostels and low-budget listings with the kind of detail on restaurants and quality hotels that independent-minded visitors on any budget might expect, whether on business in New York or trekking in Thailand. These days the guides offer recommendations from shoestring to luxury and cover a large number of destinations around the globe, including almost every country in the Americas and Europe, more than half of Africa, and most of Asia and Australasia. Rough Guides now publish:

• Travel guides to more than 200 worldwide destinations
• Dictionary phrasebooks to 22 major languages
• Maps printed on rip-proof and waterproof Polyart™ paper
• Music guides running the gamut from Opera to Elvis
• Reference books on topics as diverse as the Weather and Shakespeare
• World Music CDs in association with World Music Network.

Visit **www.roughguides.com** to see our latest publications.

Publishing information

This 1st edition published October 2005 by
Rough Guides Ltd, 80 Strand, London WC2R 0RL.
345 Hudson St, 4th Floor, New York, NY 10014,
USA.

Distributed by the Penguin Group
Penguin Books Ltd, 80 Strand, London WC2R 0RL
Penguin Group (USA), 375 Hudson Street, NY
10014, USA
Penguin Group (Australia), 250 Camberwell Road,
Camberwell, Victoria 3124, Australia
Penguin Group (Canada), 10 Alcorn Avenue,
Toronto, ON M4V 1E4, Canada
Penguin Group (New Zealand), Cnr Rosedale and
Airborne Roads, Albany, Auckland, New Zealand
Typeset in Bembo and Helvetica to an original
design by Henry Iles.
Printed and bound in China

A catalogue record for this book is available from
the British Library.

ISBN 1-84353-498-3

The publishers and author have done their best
to ensure the accuracy and currency of all the
information in **Dominican Republic DIRECTIONS**;
however, they can accept no responsibility for any
loss, injury or inconvenience sustained by any
traveller as a result of information or advice con-
tained in the Guide.

1   3   5   7   9   8   6   4   2

Help us update

We've gone to a lot of effort to ensure that the first edition of **Dominican Republic DIRECTIONS** is accurate and up-to-date. However, things change – places get "discovered", opening hours are notoriously fickle, restaurants and rooms raise prices or lower standards. If you feel we've got it wrong or left something out, we'd like to know, and if you can remember the address, the price, the phone number, so much the better.

We'll credit all contributions, and send a copy of the next edition (or any other DIRECTIONS guide

or Rough Guide if you prefer) for the best letters. Everyone who writes to us and isn't already a subscriber will receive a copy of our full-colour thrice-yearly newsletter. Please mark letters: **"Dominican Republic DIRECTIONS Update"** and send to: Rough Guides, 80 Strand, London WC2R 0RL, or Rough Guides, 4th Floor, 345 Hudson St, New York, NY 10014. Or send an email to **mail@roughguides.com**.

Have your questions answered and tell others about your trip at **www.roughguides.atinfopop.com**.

Rough Guide credits

Text editor: AnneLise Sorensen
Layout: Diana Jarvis
Photography: Demetrio Carrasco
Cartography: Jasbir Sandhu
Picture editor: Mark Thomas

Proofreader: Diane Margolis
Production: Julia Bovis
Design: Henry Iles
Cover design: Chloë Roberts

SMALL PRINT

The author

Sean Harvey was born in Kentucky, raised in Chicago and lives in New York City. He spent several years travelling as a freelance musician. He first visited the island of Hispaniola in 1990, during which he taught music in Port-au-Prince, Haiti, travelled extensively throughout the Dominican Republic and cultivated a lifelong addiction to the island and its people.

Acknowledgements

Many thanks to Lynn Guitar, Leidy Medina, Rich Weber, the Dominican list, Tim Hall, Severino Polanco and especially my wife Tory Dent.

Photo credits

Index

Maps are marked in colour.

INDEX

INDEX

DIRECTIONS on Screen

Put the guide on your computer or PDA

ROUGH GUIDES

Dominican Republic

PASSWORD PROTECTED
The contents of this CD cannot be downloaded without the book.

Full text of the guide with weblinks
For PCs, Macs, and all PDAs including Palm Pilots and Pocket PCs. The Adobe PDF version is on this CD; other formats are available as free downloads from the web.

DIRECTIONS

This mini-CD contains the complete
Dominican Republic DIRECTIONS
in Adobe PDF format, complete with maps and illustrations. PDFs are readable on any Windows or Mac-OS computer (including laptops). The mini-CD also contains instructions for further free downloads formatted for Pocket PC and Palm.

Insert the mini-CD in the central recess of any tray-loading CD-Rom drive: full instructions supplied. Note: mini-CDs will not work in slot-loading drives. Slot-loading drive owners or DIRECTIONS purchasers who have mislaid their mini-CD should go to www.directionsguides.com to download files as required. Note on platforms: Adobe supports maps and illustrations and is compatible with Mac and PC operating systems. Pocket PC and Palm platforms support text only.

www.directionsguides.com

DIRECTIONS

Algarve
1843534193

Amsterdam
1843533065

Antigua & Barbuda
1843533197

Athens
1843533146

Barbados
1843533200

Barcelona
1843533952

Costa Brava
1843534398

Lisbon
1843533154

London
1843533162

Madrid
184353410X

Marrakesh
1843533219

New Orleans
1843533936

New York City
1843533227

Paris
1843533170

Prague
1843534258

Rome

San Francisco

Tenerife & La Gomera

Venice

Washington DC

COMING SOON

US$10.99   Can$15.99   £6.99

www.directionsguides.com